Tales from the

Virginia Tech
S i d e l i n e

Chris Colston

SP
SPORTS
PUBLISHING
L.L.C.

SportsPublishingLLC.com

ISBN-13: 978-1-59670-251-6
ISBN: 1-58261-728-7 (hard cover)

Front cover photo courtesy of David Knachel/Virginia Tech

All interior photos courtesy of Virginia Tech unless otherwise noted.

Publishers: Peter L. Bannon and Joseph J. Bannon Sr.
Senior managing editor: Susan M. Moyer
Acquisitions editors: Bob Snodgrass and John Humenik
Developmental editor: Laura E. Podeschi
Art director: Dustin J. Hubbart
Cover design: Dustin J. Hubbart
Interior layout: Nancy Routh
Photo editor: Erin Linden-Levy

Sports Publishing L.L.C.
804 North Neil Street
Champaign, IL 61820
Phone: 1-877-424-2665
Fax: 217-363-2073
www.SportsPublishingLLC.com

Printed in the United States of America

Library of Congress Cataloging-in-Publication Data

Colston, Chris.
Tales from the Virginia Tech sideline / Chris Colston.
    p. cm.
  ISBN 978-1-59670-251-6 (soft cover : alk. paper) --
  ISBN 978-1-58261-728-2 (hard cover : alk. paper)
  1. Virginia Tech Hokies (Football team)--History. I. Title.
GV958.V54C657 2007
796.332'6309755785--dc22
                              2007021377

CONTENTS

ACKNOWLEDGMENTS

First and foremost, many heartfelt thanks to Virginia Tech football coach Frank Beamer and his program's heart and soul, John Ballein. Their cooperation and generosity made this book possible.

Special thanks also go to John Moody and his family: wife Kaye, and children, John, Ged, and Meg. As neighbors in the early 1970s, they first exposed my family to the Hokie football experience.

Also many thanks to all of the people who contributed their time to this project: Bill Roth, Mike Burnop, Dave Smith, David Knachel, Anne Panella, Donna Smith, Bryan Johnston, Jerr Rosenbaum, John Hunt, Mike Ashley, Lester Karlin, Billy Hite, Kevin Rogers, Don Divers, Jack Prater, Dickie and Wanda Beard (especially for the delicious cherry pie), Sean Donnelly, Stuart Plank, David Everett, Sharon McCloskey, Jack Bogaczyk ("the man who knows where all the bodies are buried"), Blair Kerkhoff, Ken Haines, Mike Harris, John Markon, Jimmy Robertson, Matt Spiers, Jeff Charles, Diana Clarke, Steve Colston, Doug Doughty, Greg Shockley, Skip Wood, Lisa Marie, Mickey Fitzgerald, J.C. Price, Carter Wiley, Tim Harvey, Harvey Laney, David Teel, Mike Shaver, Russ McCubbin, Bruce Garnes, Aaron Rouse, Bryan Stinespring, Charley Wiles, Carter Wiley, Mike Gentry, Jim Cavanaugh, Tony Ball, Lorenzo Ward, Danny Pearman, Bud Foster, Darryl Tapp, Kevin Jones, Jeff King, Will Montgomery and Bill Brill.

Thanks also to *USA TODAY*'s Monte Lorell, Lee Ivory, and Tim McQuay for giving their blessing to this project.

As always, thank you to Melanie for your patience and love.

AUTHOR'S NOTE

Virginia Tech is an underdog university accustomed to adversity. Nobody ever said being a Hokie was going to be easy. It always seems to be like that. In 1999, Tech football fans could not completely revel in the glory of an undefeated season, because the results of a Nebraska-Colorado game could still determine whether the Hokies went to the championship game. The greatest player in school history, Michael Vick, left the program with two years of eligibility on the table. In 2000, Tech had a national TV game canceled because of lightning. Even in the year it won its first bowl, 1986, head coach Bill Dooley sued his own school for $3.5 million.

Perhaps it is all to be expected, since this is a university with two nicknames, one of which is a turkey, and the other a figment of one student's imagination.

Then again, there are plusses: the colors, burnt orange and maroon, are the hues of good barbecue, Hokie Stone is a glorious building material, and the stadium public address system actually gobbles.

Oh, and does Metallica's "Enter Sandman" get the adrenaline pumping!

This paperback version of *Tales From the Virginia Tech Sideline* features an all-new final chapter, chronicling the Hokies' admittance into the ACC and their 2004 football championship season. What a joy to relive that magical run.

The problem with this book was not finding stories. Rather, it was deciding where to start. And since I have found, through years of journalistic experience, that it is extremely difficult to interview the dead, I elected to limit my interviews to those still living. Hence the bulk of this book deals with the "modern" era of Virginia Tech football.

This is not to denigrate the importance of Fighting Gobbler glory prior to the 1950s. From the university's first football game on

Friday, October 21, 1892, against St. Albans (a 14-10 Tech victory), there were, no doubt, hundreds of colorful stories. We have included a handful of them here.

Instead this book is heavy on Beamer-era lore. Considering Virginia Tech has enjoyed its greatest football success during his tenure, I hope this is not taken as an offense. Even then, I know we have barely scratched the surface.

Chris Colston
March 9, 2007

CHRIS COLSTON covers the NFL for *USA TODAY*. A 1980 graduate of Virginia Tech, he served as editor of *The Hokie Huddler* from 1985-96, where he won several national writing awards. He is the author of three books about Virginia Tech football, including *The Hokies Handbook*. He also teamed with Frank Beamer on his autobiography, *Turn Up the Wick!*

The son of Virginia Sports Hall of Famer Jim Carroll, Colston grew up in Roanoke, Virginia, and remembers when a cartoon turkey head—complete with VPI beanie cap—used to sit atop the Lane Stadium scoreboard, eyes flashing and loudly gobbling.

Today Colston lives in Oak Hill, Virginia, with his wife, Melanie, and their two children. Even though Melanie is a University of Virginia graduate, the couple has somehow managed to happily co-exist. Among other memorabilia, she even allows a cartoon turkey head—complete with VPI beanie cap—to adorn a toilet seat in their downstairs bathroom.

CHAPTER ONE

And So It All Began

In the beginning, when Virginia Tech was Virginia Agricultural & Mechanical College and its colors were black and cadet gray, the games were a disorganized frenzy with no idea of team play. Any player who found himself, by sheer dumb luck, with the ball, ran with it. The boundaries of the field were marked off with a plow. Tech's first playing field was marked off on a hill with, according to *The Bugle* yearbook, "interesting little hollows which hid the play from spectators on the other side."

In 1896 the school became Virginia Polytechnic Institute and changed its colors to Chicago maroon and burnt orange. A committee chose the colors because they made "a unique combination not worn elsewhere at the time."

Well over a century later, the committee could make the very same claim.

With its new name, VPI needed a new cheer and offered its students a prize for the best one. O.M. Stull, Class of 1896, won the contest with the now-famous chant:

Hoki, Hoki, Hoki, Hy!

Tech! Tech! VPI!
Sola-Rex Solah-Rah
Polytech Vir-gin-ia!
Rae, ri, VPI!

The word "Hoki" was simply a figment of Stull's imagination; he admitted the word had no meaning. "I thought it sounded good," he said.

It figures: the very man who invented Tech's nickname misspelled it.

Virginia Agricultural and Mechanical's very first mascot wasn't a gearshift or a turkey or a "Hoki," but a kid named Floyd Meade. He was a youth who lived with the family of cadet N.W. Thomas. At the tender age of seven, Meade became a favorite in the barracks, and cadets gave him the nickname "Hard Times."

According to Roland Lazenby's book *Legends*, Meade, as a teenager, dressed as a clown and performed at football games as a kind of one-man band. When he grew weary of that schtick, he began feeding and training a turkey that he billed as "the largest in Montgomery County."

His new act was ready for the first game of the 1912 season. He hitched his bird to a small cart and rode around the field—and in one bizarre performance, promoted both of VPI's nicknames.

Gobbler and Hokie.

The act was such a hit that Meade and his turkey appeared at VPI's annual Thanksgiving Day game. Each year he rewarded the bird by having him for dinner.

Hunter Carpenter was VPI's first football star. A member of the College Football Hall of Fame, he enrolled in 1898 at VPI as a 15-year-old freshman, waited two years, played for VPI from 1900-1903, got his degree, pursued graduate studies at North Carolina and played for the 1904 Tar Heels, then returned to VPI in 1905 as a graduate assistant—and played another season. The athletic associations back then had no firm eligibility rules; it was anarchy. Imagine the records he would have set, had they kept them.

Funny thing was that in all those years, Carpenter could never beat arch rival Virginia. He became obsessed with it, which might have had something to do with his return to Blacksburg. A few days before the November 4 showdown, Virginia officials accused VPI of paying Carpenter. The Gobblers denied the charge, but UVA said it would not play the game if Carpenter was in uniform. It was called on November 2, but VPI said it was showing up anyway. After some game-day negotiations, they reached an agreement to play.

According to *Legends*, the hotly contested game was marred by profanity and dirty play; players were taking swings and punching each other at every opportunity. It was like a University of Miami game before Larry Coker took over.

VPI won the game 11-0, but the bad blood lingered, and the two schools would not play each other again for 17 years.

Herb Thomas, who lettered in 1938-40, was another great hero from VPI's early years. He was the school's scoring leader at the turn of the decade but will always be remembered for his bravery on the battlefield.

A marine sergeant in the Pacific during World War II, Thomas was leading a group of nine men against a Japanese pillbox on Bougainville Island when a hand grenade dropped into their foxhole. Thomas threw himself on the live grenade, saving the lives of his men. He was awarded the Medal of Honor posthumously. He also won the Navy Cross. A community hospital in South Charleston, West Virginia, was named for him, as were a dormitory on Tech's campus and a USS destroyer built in 1945. His portrait hangs in the Third Marine Headquarters in Hawaii.

CHAPTER TWO

The Alabama Connection

When Frank O'Rear Moseley arrived in Blacksburg in 1950, one of his main goals was weeding out the weak. A college roommate, briefly, of the legendary Paul "Bear" Bryant at Alabama in the early 1930s, Moseley figured he'd run a practice so grueling that only the meanest would survive. He called his new regime "Operation Bootstrap."

Moseley inherited a program that had won one game in three years. Tech was a military school, and the hard ex-GIs in the stands didn't ask for much. "If we score a touchdown, we'll take a drink," they said. When scoring proved to be too great a task, they said, "Hell, if we get a first down, we'll take a drink!"

The facilities were terrible and the players not much better. "At present, we have about 50 freshmen, sophomores and juniors on football scholarships," he wrote in his first exclusive student aid association newsletter, "and in my way of thinking, only 21 of the 50 have any possibilities at all."

That first season, in 1951, recalled center-linebacker Jack Prater, was "like a war, and we were the survivors."

1954 team photo.

In those first three seasons, Moseley's teams won 12 games, but had a breakout season in 1954, when Tech went 8-0-1 and finished ranked No. 16 in the nation.

Midway through that season the spunky Hokies caught the eye of legendary *Washington Post* columnist Shirley Povich, who adopted them as his team. "Oklahoma, No. 1 you may have," he wrote. "Take Notre Dame, and UCLA and Purdue and Maryland and the other giants of college football as well. I'm choosing to suffer it out with my new heroes, the boys of VPI."

The Hokies' first game of the 1954 season was against North Carolina State, which ran a single-wing offense, a rarity even then. Frank Moseley scheduled a preseason scrimmage in Hickory, North Carolina, against Lenoir-Rhyne College, because it, too, ran the single wing.

While one Tech platoon scrimmaged the Bears, the other two ran sprints on an adjoining field.

After practice, one of the Lenoir-Rhyne players walked off the field with Jack Prater.

"What did you guys do to upset your coach?" he asked.

"Nothing," Prater said. "Why?"

"He had you running all afternoon. It looked like punishment to me."

"Hell, we do that every day," Prater said. "You mean you guys don't do that?"

The Bears' player shook his head. "What, are you crazy?"

After a decade of cheapness and futility, the Hokie football program needed a tough nut like Frank Moseley, a man who didn't give a damn about what other people thought.

"He wasn't trying to impress any [bleeping] body," said back Don Divers. "He wasn't one to put on a show."

Said running back Dickie Beard, "he never mentioned his playing days at Alabama or coaching under the Bear at Maryland and Kentucky. When he got here, he was committed to Virginia Tech."

Moseley figured the key to a successful team was conditioning. Even before games, he would only give his players a meal of toast, honey and tea. "When the game was over," said lineman Jack Prater, "our bodies would be shaking, we were so hungry."

End John Moody got married while he was still in college. "I had a heck of a lot easier time telling my parents than Coach Moseley," he said. "He wanted to know, 'How come?'"

Said Prater, "Let's put in this way. Before a game, when you were traveling, you wanted to hide your face. You just wanted to sleep. You didn't want to smile, laugh or make any kind of noise, and you didn't want to look at anybody. Because you knew damn good and well them beady eyes were looking at you."

During Tech's undefeated 1954 season, it beat Wake Forest 32-0 in Richmond's Tobacco Bowl. Moseley said the players didn't have to return on the team bus, but there was a team meeting at 2 p.m. Sunday, followed by practice.

Don Divers and Grover Jones stayed overnight in Richmond and went to church the following morning. They had no car, so they started thumbing their way back to Blacksburg. It rained, they got soaked, but they found a ride to Roanoke, where Divers called his father, who took them the rest of the way. Divers and Jones were quite late and scared to death; when they finally arrived on campus, the Tech players were just coming off the field. They went to see assistant coach Alf Satterfield, a reasonable man who acted as Moseley's buffer. Satterfield went to Moseley on their behalf and returned with bad news.

"You're off the team," he said.

On Tuesday, the team took a vote and reinstated both players. They had learned their lesson, and it was a simple one: Don't go to church!

Luke Lindon, Tech's legendary equipment manager, was a big, gruff mountain of man, one of those hard old boys from the eastern Kentucky hills. He played tackle for the University of Kentucky and was invited to the 1939 Blue-Gray game.

During one off-season, Lindon took a break from cleaning helmets. Madison "Buzz" Nutter, a lineman who became the first Tech player ever selected in the NFL draft, ambled down the hall and saw Lindon, leaning his arms on the bottom half of a two-piece swinging door. "Taking another break again, big Luke?" he said, or something to that effect.

Lindon was like a sleeping dog that came alive. He snapped the bottom half of that door open, grabbed Nutter by the collar and with one hand slung him across the room into the stack of helmets.

Then he loomed over him, pointed and said, "Listen, boy."

Nutter, who played 12 years with the Baltimore Colts, never messed with Lindon again.

The Washington Redskins actually drafted Buzz Nutter, but cut him after six games—perhaps because he was too tall (6-foot-4) for 5-foot-7 quarterback Eddie LeBaron.

"Eddie had to reach UP to get the snap from me," Nutter said when he was inducted into the Tech Sports Hall of Fame in 1985.

Moseley started the modern era of Tech football, although here, the term "modern" is used loosely. Money was still tight—there had been no fund-raising until Mose arrived—and Lindon was stingy with the new equipment.

In August 1952, John Moody asked Lindon for a pair of cleats.

"What size you wear?" Lindon asked.

Moody told him, "Seven and a half."

"Seven and a half? Hell, boy, you ain't big enough to play football," Lindon growled, throwing him the shoes. "Lookit little Bobby Scruggs. Even HE wears a size eight and a half."

A week later, Moody got a message that Luke wanted to see him. "Ah, hell, what have I done now," he thought as he went downstairs.

Lindon tossed Moody a new pair of shoulder pads, hip pads and a helmet.

"I see where you kind of like to hit people," Lindon said.

Dickie Beard, "the Cumberland Flash," was an honorable mention All-American and was named AP Athlete of the Year in Virginia. He also had a sideline habit of sucking on a lemon when he was thirsty. He was one of Moseley's favorite players, but even he incurred the coach's wrath after a disappointing 7-7 tie to Richmond in 1955.

After the game Moseley began ranting, counting off all of the Hokies' mistakes. This went on for several minutes, then Moseley finally pointed at Beard. "I'm on the sideline, looking for my captain," the coach screamed, "and there he is, taping his ankle!" Moseley began hopping around on one foot, his tie flying up into his wild, greasy hair. The players did everything they could not to laugh out loud. "Later on I'm looking for my captain, and there he is, standing on the sideline, sucking on a lemon!" And Moseley held the imaginary fruit up and began pounding his mouth with such force, said Prater, "he almost knocked out his teeth."

The whole team was doubled over, afraid to laugh, and the seething Moseley screamed, "What did you have in there, Beard? Your lunch?"

Carroll Dale was Virginia Tech's first All-American and one of the greatest players in school history. The September 7, 1957 edition of the *Saturday Evening Post* named him the top sophomore lineman in the nation. After his junior season he was named the Southern Conference Player of the Year. His senior year he was named first-team All-America by *Look* magazine. He achieved all of these honors despite a career where he was often double- and triple-teamed.

The Los Angeles Rams drafted him in 1960 and he caught a touchdown pass in his first pro game. After five seasons with the Rams he was traded to Green Bay, where he was a starter on three consecutive championship teams under Vince Lombardi. He was named to the Pro Bowl in 1970 and 1971.

Dale retired in the late 1970s and returned to the coal fields of his youth, where he owned and operated a strip-mining company.

According to Roland Lazenby's book *Legends*, a Roanoke newspaper tracked down Dale in Pound, Virginia. He found him enjoying the hard work of mining. "After playing in the dirt for 23 years, if I'd sit down I'd have a health problem," he told the reporter. "I just cannot stand to be a spectator."

In 1957, for the season opener, Tech took a train to New Orleans to play Tulane. The Hokies won 14-13, and Moseley announced a 1 a.m. curfew. But when nobody had knocked on their doors by 2 a.m., most of the players sneaked back out on the street again. John Moody's suite-mate, John "Head" Herndon, had gotten very little sleep that night. (They called him "Head" because, to be honest, he had a really large head.) Moseley was big on doing things as a group, and everybody was expected to eat together. But Moody couldn't wake Herndon. One of their teammates knocked on the door and peeked in.

Carroll Dale.

"You guys OK?" he said. "You better hurry or you're going to be late for breakfast."

Pity the man who faced Moseley's wrath, so Moody and his cohorts left Herndon, who promptly flopped backwards on the bed and resumed snoring.

Moseley counted heads and realized he was missing "Head." That's about when Herndon appeared, wearing Moody's pants, which he had groggily grabbed. They were about three sizes too short.

When the team returned to Blacksburg, Moseley called a team meeting, where he ranted and raved about being on time and ordered a vote on whether Herndon should stay on the team. Either way, Moseley said, he was taking away Herndon's scholarship.

The players voted to keep him and then chipped in their monthly laundry money ($10) to help Herndon, who was married, make ends meet. Their generosity kept Herndon, a brilliant student, in school, and he earned his degree.

"Head" went on to become a brain surgeon.

Few Hokie fans probably remember a lineman named Bobby "Baby" Seal, who lettered just one season (1952). But his teammates will never forget him. "He looked like Lou Costello," Divers said. "He had round shoulders, was very pigeon-toed, and kind of waddled when he walked. But he wasn't a bad football player."

Divers recalled one afternoon when several of the players were hanging out in Baby Seal's room. He was sitting quietly on his top bunk, and said, "I wish I was that pair of shoes on the floor."

"Why is that?" Divers said.

"Because then I could lay there all day and never have to move," he said.

Seal was a good high-school wrestler, and one year Tech wrestling coach Frank Teske was short a heavyweight. "I need you against Virginia," he told Seal. "I need a heavyweight."

Seal wasn't enamored with the idea, but agreed to do it. What he didn't know was that the Cavaliers' heavyweight was a fellow by the name of Henry Jordan—the same mean, strong son of a gun who was inducted into the NFL Hall of Fame in 1995.

Jordan took Baby Seal down in short order, mashing his face into the mat. When the match was over, Baby Seal went to Coach Teske.

"I'm not wrasslin' any more," he said.

In 1956 there was a joke going around campus about two brothers in a pickup truck who stole a pig. The police pulled them over, so the boys quickly placed the pig between them and put a hat on its head. The policeman shined his light into the cab and asked the driver's name. "Joe Anderson," he said. Then he asked the other one's name. "Bill Anderson," he said.

"And you short fella in the middle," the cop said. "What's your name?"

Joe Anderson poked the pig in the ribs. "Oink!" he said.

"OK," the cop said. "You're free to go." Then he went back to his patrol car and turned to his partner. "That Oink Anderson," he said, "is about the ugliest man I've ever seen."

While this joke made its rounds, Bob McCoy showed up at a dance with his date.

"Hey, look!" teammated Billy Holsclaw yelled from across the room. "Bobby brought along one o' them ANDERSON girls!"

You won't find his name among the lettermen in the *Maroon Book*, but Julian Russell McCubbin was one of Virginia Tech's all-time most colorful players. Born in Charleston, West Virginia, he starred at Hargrave Military Academy and earned a Fighting Gobbler scholarship. He stayed in Blacksburg from 1953-54 before entering the U.S. Army.

McCubbin was handsome, friendly, outgoing, cocky—and a heck of a street fighter. "He had lots of charisma," teammate Don Divers said. "From the waist up, he looked like a body builder, even though few players used weights in that era."

McCubbin liked to wear fancy clothes and he even owned a pair of pink pants. He used to walk into Don Divers' room—he always kept it very neat—open a drawer, take out a brush, look in the mirror and make a big production of combing his hair.

"Divers," he said, "you ever seen anything like this?" and he would start flexing his muscles. "I'm about the prettiest thing you've ever seen, except for my damn bird legs."

The freshman team played a four-game schedule, including a trip to Duke. The Blue Devils had a quarterback named Sonny Jurgensen and a highly recruited guard named Roy Hord Jr. whom everybody touted as a sure-fire All-American. Duke won the game, but McCubbin had beaten Hord all over the field. Around the third quarter, he looked at Hord.

"Son, if you're All-American," he said, "then what do you think I ought to be?"

When McCubbin's tour of duty was over, he returned to Blacksburg, briefly, in 1957. Legend has it that Moseley was putting his players through a typically brutal practice when McCubbin decided he had enough and started to walk off the field.

"Hey, McCubbin! Where you goin'?" Moseley yelled at him.

"Coach," he said, "I'm goin' to Hollywood."

McCubbin denied the story. "I came back to Blacksburg," he said, "and the first night, somebody broke into my car and stole all my clothes. I had some nice clothes made, too, and a really nice tweed coat like the kind George Preas used to wear. Well, that didn't sit too well with me. I had an idea who stole them, but I couldn't prove it. It was then I realized that I had lost my desire to play, and I got the wanderlust. So I headed to Florida for a while before I ended up in Hollywood."

After hitch-hiking to Los Angeles, he made the rounds of agents by day and parked cars at night. There was a big photo spread in *Life* magazine, 15 half-naked men in a tree, all vying to become the next Tarzan. McCubbin was one of them, but didn't get the part. Maybe his legs were too skinny.

He became a regular on television, working as Clint Walker's stand-in on *Cheyenne*. The two became close and still keep in touch. "I called him on the phone when he turned 76," McCubbin said, "and I sang 'Happy Birthday to You.'"

Clint Eastwood and Russell McCubbin. *Photo courtesy of Russell McCubbin*

Through the years he made guest appearances on *Gunsmoke, Tarzan, Laredo, Daniel Boone, Magnum, P.I., Dukes of Hazzard, The Wild Wild West, Adam-12, Marcus Welby, M.D.* and many others.

He appeared in 15 movies, including *Another 48 Hours, Sudden Impact, Any Which Way You Can, High Plains Drifter* and *Myra Breckenridge.*

"I met John Wayne, Gary Cooper, Clark Gable," he said. When asked what Wayne was like, he said, "He wore lifts in his shoes, and he wore a hairpiece. He was a good fella. Well, people either liked him or they didn't. He hollered and spat tobacco. I got along with him fine."

He also had leading roles in the plays *Send Me No Flowers, Bus Stop, A Spring to Remember, Tea and Sympathy* and others. He also starred in several commercials, including ones for Miller Beer and Burger King.

According to friends, McCubbin woke up one morning in 1992 and thought, "You know, if I die out here, I'll have to pay for my pallbearers." He packed his bags and returned to West Virginia, where for the last decade he has performed as a stand-up comic. He has a website, russmccubbin.com.

The old Hokie is one comedian you don't want to heckle. "People say that if someone hoots at him, he won't think twice of challenging someone in the crowd," Divers said. "He'll point at you and say, 'Buddy, I'll take you outside,' and he's not joking then."

As a Richmond prepster, John Moody had received several scholarship offers and had actually signed with Washington & Lee. He came from a middle-class family and owned one sport coat and two ties, so when he learned that coat and tie was de rigueur at W&L, well, that posed a bit of a problem. Upon further investigation he learned that weekly costs for a student at the school averaged about $50. "Good Lord," he said.

He took another look at Virginia Tech, which was still an all-military school then and the school would give him clothes. Sure, it was a cadet uniform, but he didn't have to worry about that $50 a week either.

"It's amazing how the smallest things can dictate a decision that impacts you for the rest of your life," Moody said.

A few months before Frank Moseley arrived in Blacksburg, Virginia Tech dropped its opposition to athletics fund-raising. A group headed by Red English and E.R. Lane formed the Virginia Tech Student Aid Foundation in 1949-50. The group raised $10,000 and was eager to present the cash to Moseley during a special gathering at a Roanoke hotel.

"I got up in front of the group and gave my little song and dance about how hard we had worked for it," English said in Legends. "When I got through, Moseley said, 'If that's all you got, just keep it.' He shocked that crowd into giving another $9,000 more that night."

In 1972, Virginia Tech Student Aid director (and former Tech coach) Mac McEver hired John Moody as fund-raiser. A few years later, through the Frank Moseley-Jimmy Sharpe-Alabama connection, the Hokie Club had booked Bear Bryant as a banquet speaker. Before dinner, Moseley and Moody held a happy hour in their hotel suite.

Moody was tending bar and asked the legendary Bear if he would like a drink.

"Believe I do," he said.

Moody fixed him a scotch and water. Three minutes later, the Bear returned. "Coach, would you like another one?" Moody asked.

"Yep," he said. Moody poured him one, and the Bear stared at it.

"What's a matter, boy?" he said. "You runnin' out a scotch?"

"Here, Coach," Moody said, respectfully pushing him the bottle. "You fix it just how you like it!"

It took Bryant a little longer to finish that drink, but he returned to the bar, where he found Moody packing things up; the banquet was about to start. Moody looked up, startled.

"Hey, Coach," he said. "Would you like another drink?"

"Believe I do."

Moody pulled out the scotch and Bryant filled his glass again.

When Moody arrived at the civic center, a string orchestra was playing and dinner was ready to start. McEver confronted him. "Where's Mose and Coach Bryant?"

"They were still in the suite when I left," Moody said.

"You get on the phone and tell them to get their [bleeping] asses over here," McEver said.

"Coach, I'll call and tell them we're ready to start," Moody said, "but if you want it told like that, you'll have to call them yourself." Just about that time Bryant and Moseley walked in the door. Big Luke Lindon, who played for Bryant at Kentucky, came up to shake the Bear's hand. Bryant took his hand and waltzed Lindon across the floor, cracking everybody up.

"Go fix Coach Bryant a plate," McEver told Moody. "That's easy; I can handle that," Moody thought, and piled it high so Bryant would get something besides scotch in his stomach.

When it came time for his speech, the Bear began his signature mumbling. "Oh Lord," Moody said, "I'm going to lose my job. They're going to blame me for over-serving him."

Then Bryant told the classic "Timbuktu" joke, which has many iterations, but one version goes something like this:

The two finalists in a national poetry contest were a Hokie and an Alabama graduate. The Bama graduate went first and was given one word to turn into a poem. His word was "Timbuktu." He thought for a moment, then started:

"Across the burning desert sands, trekked a camel caravan, men and camels two by two, destination Timbuktu." Everyone was duly impressed and then the Hokie was given the same word, "Timbuktu." The Hokie thought for while and finally stood and said, "Me and Tim a-hunting went, we saw three damsels in a tent. They were three and we were two, so I bucked one and Tim bucked two."

Well, the whole place roared. "Bryant went on to give one of the greatest speeches I've ever heard," Moody said, "and I kept my job."

Mac McEver and Frank Moseley were good friends, but they had their disagreements. "Mac's office was directly over Mose's office," John Moody said. "You could be outside and hear them arguing about something, and then Mac would stomp upstairs. When that happened, you knew better than to go visit him. You waited for him to call you."

In the 1960s, Frank Moseley realized he had to devote more time to his duties as athletic director and began a search for his successor. He turned to his old mentor, Bear Bryant, and plucked one of his minions.

Jerry Claiborne (10 seasons as Tech head coach, 61-39-2 overall from 1961-70) played on Bryant's Kentucky teams in the 1940s, when Moseley was an assistant. He knew all about Claiborne's determination and will. He was Bryant's defensive coach at Texas A&M, and in 1956 the Aggies were ranked No. 8 nationally in total defense. The following year Frank Broyles, then at Missouri, hired Claiborne, and he devised a pass defense that ranked No. 2 nationally. As Bryant's defensive coordinator in 1958 and 1959, the Crimson Tide led the nation in pass defense.

If the Hokies were not going to hire a proven head coach, then Claiborne had the best credentials for assistant that they were going to find.

Like Moseley, Claiborne was a no-nonsense guy; he told you straight up where you stood, and he didn't play favorites.

Even to Frank Beamer.

It was 1969, and Beamer was teaching math at Radford High School. He had picked up a copy of the *Roanoke Times*, where Bill Brill had written a column about the local semipro football team, the Roanoke Buckskins. Brill suggested the club bring in some local flavor like former Hokies Beamer and Ron Davidson. Beamer thought Brill's idea had merit, so he went to go see Coach Claiborne.

"This article has got me thinking," he said. "Do you reckon I should go up to Roanoke and try to play semipro ball?"

Claiborne stared at him. He had a hard stare. "Frank," he said. "I've seen you run. I've seen you play. If I were you, I'd get on with my life's work."

Many fans, when you say the words "Jerry Claiborne," immediately think of Frank Loria.

Loria, little No. 10, wasn't big (5'9", 175) or fast (4.7 in the forty), but he was Tech's first consensus All-American, making the squad twice and also being named an Academic All-American. What he lacked in natural physical ability he more than made up for in toughness.

"We had a footwork drill in practice where you would step through ropes," said teammate Frank Beamer. "He'd cross up his feet and trip and fall. You watched him do that drill and your first thought was for his personal safety."

As great as he was, Loria went undrafted. He became defensive coordinator at Marshall and died November 14, 1970, when the Thundering Herd team plane crashed short of the Huntington airport runway.

Those who knew him believed Loria would have been a great coach. Someone once asked Frank Beamer, "If Frank Loria were still alive, would he be coaching for you?"

"If Frankie was still here," Beamer said, "I might be coaching for him."

The late Sonny Utz was a bruising fullback under Claiborne. He was "Mr. Inside" to Bob Schweickert's "Mr. Outside." Utz was a great football player who used to tackle cows for fun, but he hated to study.

Coach Jerry Claiborne.

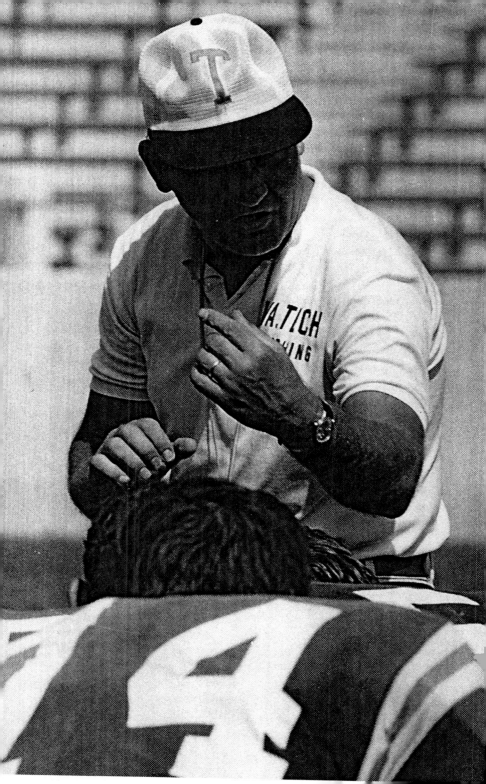

One night his roommate, Tommy Walker, tried to convince Utz to study for a big test the following day. As usual, Utz was in no mood for academia. In the dormitory hallway, a couple of guys were having a water-balloon battle, and despite Walker's protests, Utz was gone.

He returned with a trash can brimming with water, dumped it over Walker's head, and fled.

Walker grabbed the trash can, filled it and sprinted into the hallway, sloshing water as he went, but everyone was gone—except one man.

Doug Shively, one of Claiborne's assistant coaches.

Some fans weren't thrilled with Jerry Claiborne's conservative style—he was Bill Dooley before Bill Dooley—but he led the Hokies to their first legitimate bowl bids. True, Tech earned a bid to the 1947 Sun Bowl with a 3-3-3 regular-season mark, but that was only because a prominent Tech alumnus on the bowl committee exerted a little favoritism.

The Hokies faced Miami in the 1966 Liberty Bowl. During the team luncheon, officials gave each Tech player a beautiful watch, where every 30 seconds or so a picture of the Liberty Bowl would appear on the face. "Man, this is cool," the players thought. "What a big-time watch." Everyone was admiring his new gift when, from the middle of the room, one of the players said, "Hey, my watch just stopped!"

A few seconds later, someone said, "Hey, now mine just stopped!"

This went on for the next two, three, five, ten minutes: people saying, "My watch just stopped." Players were taking bets on whose watch would stop next.

Frank Loria (fourth from left) shown here with fellow Liberty Bowl-bound Tech players.

CHAPTER THREE

The '70s

For Virginia Tech football, the 1970s were a time when you could sit pretty much wherever you wanted in Lane Stadium. The scoreboard featured a beanie-wearing turkey whose eye flashed, and he gobbled when the Hokies scored a touchdown. Up in the corners, restless kids would pass the time stepping on ketchup packets, trying to squirt each other. There always seemed to be a pickup football game going on in the grassy area behind the north end zone. The cheerleaders wore hot pants and boots. For frigid games, vendors would roam through the aisles wearing white plastic hot chocolate dispensers on their backs. Under the stands, concessionaires sold the ubiquitous long orange horns, Cracker Jacks and pins with orange and maroon ribbons and little gold plastic footballs hanging from them.

New coach Charlie Coffey had Lane Stadium's end zones painted in orange and white checkerboards, just like at Tennessee's Neyland Stadium. He switched the jerseys from maroon to burnt orange. And he changed the helmet logo from the classic "VT" to the letters T-E-C-H stenciled over an orange rendering of the Commonwealth of Virginia. It looked great up close, but from a distance, the new logo was pretty much unintelligible.

The biggest change was in Tech's offensive approach. Under new coordinator Dan Henning, the Hokies would no longer be a conservative, run-oriented squad. The plan was a new pro-style, pass-oriented attack.

But who would trigger it? In the spring of 1971, the Hokies had three tall, talented quarterbacks: Strock, Gil Schwabe, and Bob German.

Don Strock is a Lane legend, but he almost never got the chance to show what he could do. German had been Tech's passing leader in 1969; Schwabe in 1970. That spring Henning gave all three an equal shot, and all performed evenly. The only difference was that Schwabe (pronounced "Shwob") and German were seniors, while Strock was a junior. Since the competition was a draw, Henning opted for the player with the most remaining eligibility.

Strock threw for 2,577 yards in 1971 and a school-record 3,243 yards in 1972. The Miami Dolphins drafted him in the fifth round of the '73 NFL draft.

"He threw for all those yards and set records and went on to a long pro career," said one of his favorite targets, tight end Mike Burnop. "But if he had been a rising senior that spring, he probably would have ended up coaching high school football somewhere."

Mike Burnop's single-season school receiving mark (46 catches) lasted for 31 years before Ernest Wilford caught 51 passes in 2002. Of course, Burnop set the record in 11 games, while Wilford tied Burnop in his 13th regular-season game and broke it in game No. 14, the San Francisco Bowl.

"Really, 46 catches isn't that much," Burnop said, "so it amazed me that the record stood for as long as it did."

From left: Don Strock, Wally English, and Charlie Coffey.

Burnop, a tight end, set the record in a Tech offense where he was the "hot" receiver. He would release over the middle, and Strock was tall enough (6-foot-5) to see over the line and dump it off to him as a safety valve. "I got a lot of catches like that," he said.

One problem new coach Charlie Coffey encountered upon inheriting Jerry Claiborne's squad was a paucity of wide receivers. He was so desperate that he began using student manager Kit Utz in passing drills. The coaches appreciated Utz's precise routes so much that they gave him a uniform.

Utz (pronounced the same way Joe Pesci said "youths" in the film *My Cousin Vinny*—yewtz) was no relation to Sonny Utz (pronounced how it's spelled), but like Sonny, he became a Tech letterman (1971-72).

Against Southern Miss in Lane Stadium, he had a chance for glory, but dropped a couple of touchdown passes that were right in his hands.

"He told us the sun was in his eyes," Mike Burnop said.

Today Utz coaches girls' basketball at a private school in Naples, Florida, and when the Hokies travel to Miami, Burnop always visits his old teammate.

And when he sees him, he always puts an index finger below each eye.

"Eye black!" Burnop tells him with a smile.

Kit Utz's story—water boy to ballplayer—made good copy. Burnop used to ride Utz about keeping his newspaper clipping in his wallet and pulling it out when he was trying to impress a young woman.

"Yeah, he'd keep it right next to his million-dollar bill," Burnop said. "He had this fake million-dollar bill, and thought it was the funniest thing to pull it out at the cash register and ask if they could make change."

Many years later, Utz and Burnop got together in Blacksburg for a game. Burnop's mother, who was in her nineties, witnessed Utz's favorite joke once again.

"Kit," she said, "you really need to get some new material."

During the 1970s, the university faced an identity crisis. Half of the Hokies' community referred to the school as "VPI," while the other half called it "Virginia Tech." Technically, neither was correct: the school's official name was Virginia Polytechnic Institute and State University.

It didn't end there. Some believed "Hokies" wasn't a desirable nickname, because it had negative connotations. Others preferred it to "Fighting Gobblers," because they didn't want to be called turkeys (more negative connotations).

At the 1973 NIT, network announcers interviewed head cheerleader Martha "the Head Hokie" Oakie. Broadcaster Don Criqui asked her the inevitable question: "What is a Hokie?"

Afraid she might say the wrong thing, Oakie replied, "It's an old Indian tribe."

At least she didn't say, "A castrated turkey."

Then there was the whole issue of colors. Was maroon the predominant color? Jimmy Sharpe and Bill Dooley thought so. Or was it orange? Charlie Coffey thought it was. And did you really want to put the two together? Dooley's first uniforms had only the faintest orange around the VT helmet insignia.

The dichotomies went on. Academically, the school was perceived as an agriculture school (the silos and cow fields as you entered campus didn't dampen that perception). But it had a nationally reknowned engineering program. The student body was a mix of civilians and cadets, and so there were two bands: The civilian Marching Virginians and the cadets' Highty-Tighties. The school was Independent in football, Metro Conference in other sports.

"We knew the school was marketable," said Raycom CEO Ken Haines, who was Tech's director of public affairs during the 1970s.

"A lot of the things that people perceived as negatives—the location, the nickname, the colors, the military—became positives. The thought was, 'How could this school ever be big in athletics? It's tucked away in the mountains, far from the big media centers.' But because of that, it became attractive to people who wanted to get away from all of that."

The Coffey Break lasted three seasons (1971-73). It had gotten off to an auspicious start; the very first play Charlie Coffey called was a fly pattern. Quarterback Don Strock faded back and heaved a 60-yard pass, and even though it fell incomplete, the crowd, weary of the old three-yards-and-a-cloud-of-dust philosophy, stood and cheered.

Tech went 2-9 in '73 and got waxed 77-6 at Alabama, the worst loss in school history. The Crimson Tide set an NCAA record for rushing yardage (758 yards). The next day, the local headline read: "At least nobody got killed."

So Coffey was fired and in came Jimmy Sharpe, 34, an assistant under Bear Bryant for 11 years. Sharpe ditched Coffey's orange Tennessee motif in favor of maroon, and the club went from pass-first to a wishbone attack.

Sharpe also hired one heck of a staff that included college teammate Charley Pell, former All-SEC lineman Danny Ford, and former LSU quarterback Nelson Stokely. Pell became head coach at Clemson and Florida. Ford led Clemson to a national championship.

Sharpe lasted from 1974-77. "That last year, the team was struggling, and there was talk of a replacement," said Ken Haines, who served as color analyst on the Tech radio broadcasts. "I think I said that if a change was going to be made, they would have to look outside because there was nobody on the current staff who was head coaching material."

Coach Jimmy Sharpe.

Hello, Dooley

After the back-to-back fiascos of hiring top assistants to run its football program, in 1978 Virginia Tech officials wanted a man with proven head coaching success. For years it had watched North Carolina's Bill Dooley lure many of the commonwealth's top players to Chapel Hill. He had led the Tar Heels to six bowls in 11 seasons. His coaching skills were rock-solid.

The only problem was that he wasn't necessarily looking to leave.

Tech president William Lavery enticed Dooley with the dual role of head coach and athletics director. The two-headed job would ultimately cause his downfall, but it sounded like a good offer at the time. Dooley accepted.

It was a key hire in more ways than one. The school was still experiencing an identity crisis. There was a feeling across campus that academics should come first, while others believed Virginia Tech's athletic potential was still largely untapped. The hiring of Dooley ostensibly sent out a message that the Hokies were committed to playing big-time football—but the schedule continued to feature the same old state schools such as VMI, William & Mary and Richmond, and regular non-conference foes such as Appalachian State.

"Through the early 1980s, there was that question in people's minds," said then-Hokies voice Jeff Charles, now the voice of the

Coach Bill Dooley.

East Carolina Pirates. "Are they really stepping it up, or was Bill Dooley coming here just to win games against mediocre competition? It was almost like a tug of war."

The good news was that Dooley began recruiting better players. The bad news was that he took down the flashing-eye gobbling turkey from the scoreboard.

Bill Dooley was an old-school coach and a former All-Star guard at Mississippi State. A native of Mobile, Alabama, he was the type of guy who, when frustrated, would exclaim, "Good gawd ol' Friday blues." He also had a term, "Riverside it," when he wanted somebody to go in the opposite direction. He could use this in any number of ways; for instance, if a player was injured and writhing in pain on the ground, he would say, "Well hell, boy, just rivah-side it."

One day in practice the Hokies were working on their isolation drill, where the fullback isolates on the linebacker, and the trailing tailback reads the block. The fullback failed his task miserably, and Dooley was all over him. "Well hell, boy," he said, a cigarette dangling from his lips, "you gotta hit that hole like a Mack truck."

They ran the play again and this time the linebacker put the fullback flat on his back. There was a momentary silence; everybody was anticipating a Dooley explosion.

"Well hell, boy," he drawled, "that time you looked more like a Toyota."

When new Tech head coach Bill Dooley was at North Carolina, he lost a prized recruit. The reason: the other school's cafeteria had a soft ice cream machine.

When he arrived in Blacksburg, the first item on Dooley's "To-Do" list was:

1. Install Soft Ice Cream Machine in Cafeteria.

Then-assistant sports information director Dave Smith was leaving Cassell Coliseum one afternoon in 1978 when he saw fullback Mickey Fitzgerald moping along. "What's the matter, Mickey?" he said.

"Aw, it's my birthday," he said.

"Your birthday?" Smith said. "Well, you should be happy!"

I don't know," Fitzgerald said. "One year ago today, Coach Sharpe slapped me on the back and said, 'Here, take the keys to my Bronco and do whatever you want tonight!'

"But Coach Dooley hasn't even wished me 'Happy Birthday' yet."

During his playing days, Tech tailback Mickey Fitzgerald (1976-79) was known as the Incredible Hulk. He might have been one of the greatest rushers in school history, even though he gained just 1,449 career yards.

He began his career as a tight end, but switched to fullback on Nov. 5, 1977 against No. 15 Florida State. Coach Jimmy Sharpe's club was a woeful 1-5-1 and he figured, what the hell.

The hunch worked: Fitzgerald pounded out 112 yards on 25 carries, and the Hokies nearly pulled the upset before losing 23-21.

The next week against West Virginia, Fitzgerald rushed 28 times for 144 yards, and the Hulk was loose. He had 142 yards and three scores against Wake Forest and 104 yards and three more touchdowns in the season finale against VMI. He was just getting started, but the season was over. Sharpe was fired, and in came Bill Dooley, who believed the fullback's role was to block for the tailback.

Although his glory days were over, Fitzgerald had enough talent to play professionally. He loved to travel during the off season, and while in Tai Pei, he toured the country with a befriended local. One day Fitzgerald's new friend took him to a virility ritual.

"Make me a promise," the local man said.

"In America," Fitzgerald said, "we like to know what we're promising."

"This is no American promise," he said. "This is Oriental promise."

Fitzgerald shrugged, surrendering more to curiosity than anything. "OK, I promise," he said.

"You must drink snake blood," the local man said.

Fitzgerald said nothing, as he felt nauseated.

The ritual was like something out of the film *Raiders of the Lost Ark*. The locals cut off a snake's head in front of Fitzgerald. Then they squeezed its gall bladder—"it was green and gooey," Fitzgerald said—and diluted the mixture with wine.

"They poured it all into this nasty, filthy glass," Fitzgerald said. "Suddenly I wasn't so worried about the snake blood. I was more concerned about catching hepatitis from the glass."

Mickey Fitzgerald spent six months in Japan as a sumo wrestler, training under the great Jesse Takamiyama. Takamiyama, an American from Hawaii, became the first foreigner to win a tournament when he took the 1974 Nagoya Basho championship. While in Japan, Fitzgerald met several members of the Japanese mafia. "They have a custom that they must cut off their pinky fingers to show allegiance," Fitzgerald said. "And if they ever mess up something, they must cut off another finger.

"If you try to shake hands with a guy who has nothing but a nub, then you know you've met a real screw-up."

In 1995, Mickey Fitzgerald was the subject of a *Hokie Huddler* article and sent this memorandum to the *Huddler* office:

TO: Chris Colston and Eric Major
FROM: Mickey Fitzgerald
RE: *Huddler* story

I wanted to thank both of you for your interest in me and your efforts in writing an article about my progress through the years. I look forward to reading it with great anticipation.

I have known Chris for many years and still want to wrestle him. Eric, I will have to determine if you are also wrestling material when I meet you. I hope to see both of you soon and will treat you to drinks, depending on how good the story is, of course.

In 1981, Virginia Tech was primed for its second consecutive bowl invitation under Bill Dooley. With a 6-3 mark, all the Hokies had to do was beat heavy underdog VMI in Blacksburg on November 21. The Hall of Fame Bowl was itching to make the announcement. "It was all done but the silk-screened T-shirts," said *Richmond Times-Dispatch* columnist John Markon.

ABC televised the game regionally, which was a good thing, because the weather was bitterly cold, making it difficult to pass. Since neither team was adept at that particular aspect of football, the game became a defensive struggle. Quarterback Steve Casey completed just eight of 23 passes with three interceptions. Tech had five turnovers, and a fumble led to VMI's only score. The Hokies lost 6-0.

The Hall of Fame Bowl committee kept calling the Tech press box for a score update. They called so often that members of the press corps began answering the phone.

One of Virginia Tech's most exciting wins came in 1982 at Duke against star quarterback Ben Bennett. In a regionally televised game, the Hokies fell behind 21-0 in the first half. Quarterback Todd Greenwood hit tight end Mike Shaw with a one-yard scoring pass to make it 21-7 before halftime; quarterback Mark Cox connected with Tony McKee on a 36-yard touchdown pass in the third quarter; then Greenwood hit Allan Thomas on a 49-yard scoring pass with 33 seconds remaining to bring Tech within one.

Go for the tie or the win? Dooley never hesitated, and he knew exactly what play he would call: a quick pass to Shaw. The two-point conversion was a success, and when the Blue Devils missed a last-second 52-yard field goal, the Hokies had pulled out the win.

"That pass to Shaw was Dooley's 'In Case of Fire, Break Glass' play," said *Richmond Times-Dispatch* columnist John Markon. "He said the play had never been defensed. The only time it ever failed was when the tight end dropped the ball, or the quarterback threw a bad pass."

Quarterback Todd Greenwood didn't throw a bad pass that time at Duke. But it was sort of amazing that he was throwing it at all. As a freshman he was so small that he was bounced from the weight room.

According to a story in the 1983 *Maroon Book*, Greenwood was in Blacksburg early in the summer before he was set to enroll. He decided to get in a workout while Tech was holding its annual All-Sports Camp for kids. He went into the weight room during a time reserved for varsity football players, and a big lineman, Mike Kovac, came rumbling over toward him. "No campers allowed in here right now," he said.

Every other year Tech would play VMI in the Oyster Bowl at Norfolk's Foreman Field. That came to an end in 1984, with a 54-7 Hokies win. The stadium's ancient locker room was experiencing a bit of a plumbing problem, as there were nearly six inches of water standing on the floor. Dooley answered the postgame media questions at the door of the locker room, in his bare feet, water above his ankles, as the reporters stood outside.

"I don't think," he said in his trademark deliberate manner, "that we will be returning to the Oyster Bowl."

There was a chilly forecast for Tech and Virginia's 1982 Thanksgiving night game in Blacksburg, so offensive coordinator Pat Watson instructed equipment manager Lester Karlin to head to Kmart. Karlin asked him why.

To buy a boatload of pantyhose, Watson said.

Well, OK, Karlin said. He bought every pack of queen-sized hose he could find and dozens of work gloves.

"I wore a pair, too," Karlin said. "Those pantyhose kept you warm."

Smith pulled on the pantyhose and came up to the equipment counter, and defensive tackle James Patterson was right behind him.

"I know I look good," Smith said to Patterson, "but quit looking at my butt."

Outland Trophy.

NFL sackmaster Bruce Smith became the first football player from a Virginia school to win the Outland Trophy. In four years at Virginia Tech, Smith accounted for losses totaling more than five times the length of a football field (504 yards).

Many people, however, will always remember Smith for the 1984 Independence Bowl fiasco. A year and a half earlier, the NCAA ruled Smith and seven other players ineligible for postseason play because of rules infractions. Despite a 9-2 record, the Hokies did not go bowling in 1983, so the point was moot.

But when they got the '84 Independence bid, it was moot no more. The other seven players were cleared after appeals, but not Smith. During the recruiting process a Tech coach had made an illegal contact with Smith, and an alumnus had sent a load of firewood to Smith's father.

"There's got to be more to it than that," *Richmond Times-Dispatch* columnist John Markon said to assistant coach Tom Fletcher. "You can't tell me all this is about some wormy old wood."

We're not sure whether he was joking or not when he said to Markon, "Sometimes, it's not the firewood, but the truck it comes in on."

Head coach Bill Dooley knew about Bruce Smith's postseason status but chose to keep it quiet. So when the story broke, it was big news. Would the Independence Bowl have tendered Tech the offer if it knew Smith would not play? Why wasn't anybody told?

Smith took the case to court. He claimed he had done nothing wrong and that he deserved to play in his first—and only—bowl game. Judge Kenneth Devore ruled in favor of Smith. The NCAA was irate and threatened to pull its sanction from the game. The next day bowl chairman Dr. Cecil Lloyd wrote a letter to the NCAA saying it would abide by the NCAA's edict.

So Smith filed another suit, this time in Caddo Parish Circuit Court in Shreveport, Louisiana. This went on all week. "Smith spent as much time at Caddo Parish Courthouse as he did at the team hotel or the practice field," said then-*Roanoke Times* writer Jack Bogaczyk. The judge agreed that Smith had not been given due process and should be allowed to play.

The NCAA urged the Independence Bowl to take the matter to a Louisiana Court of Appeals, but the three-judge panel refused to hear any arguments. The panel's ruling said, in part: "The original violations were relatively minor, the probationary sanctions directed at the school have long since expired, the sanctions against other Virginia Tech athletes were removed, and Smith is the only athlete in the entire country singled out as ineligible for postseason play."

In the parking lot outside of the courthouse, a group of reporters waited for Dooley and Tech president William Lavery.

Norfolk Virginian-Pilot executive sports editor George McClelland confronted the two.

Said then-*News-Messenger* sports editor Harvey Laney, "It was almost like a Dennis Miller-type rant. He was a tightly wound man and his frustration over the whole fiasco bubbled over."

It was the beginning of the end for Dooley at Virginia Tech. "It was never the same for Dooley and the program after that," Bogaczyk said.

Said Laney, "I think everybody who witnessed the confrontation got the feeling that, from that moment, Dooley's days at Tech were numbered."

The game itself was an anticlimax. Smith played awfully, his teammates weren't much better, and the much smaller, more focused Air Force team won easily 23-7.

The next morning, Hokies broadcaster Jeff Charles went for an early-morning run. When he returned to the hotel, he saw star defensive end Jesse Penn walking aimlessly around the parking lot, kicking pieces of gravel. "What's wrong?" Charles asked him.

"I can't believe we let those little guys beat us," Penn said.

Bruce Smith has always been an articulate speaker, even before being swamped for interviews during his college career. The problem for sports information director Jack Williams wasn't the interview itself; it was getting Smith there on time.

In 1984, Sally Jenkins of the *Washington Post* arrived for her Smith interview a few minutes early. "Bruce will be here any minute," Williams told her.

That's when assistant director Dave Smith looked through the window and saw Smith outside, in sweats, jogging around the baseball field.

Smith waved Williams into his office. "Uh, Jack," he said, "you might want to tell her Bruce will be a little late."

Defensive end Bruce Smith.

During the early 1980s, Ashley Lee was one of Virginia Tech's great players. Until his senior year, when he moved to safety, the 6-foot-1 Lee played linebacker, even though he weighed less than 200 pounds. In 1981 he led the team with 146 tackles.

"He was actually better as a linebacker," said *Richmond Times-Dispatch* columnist John Markon, "even though he had a nearly terminal lack of size."

One day Lee was sitting in assistant coach Tom Fletcher's office. "Ashley," Fletcher said, "it's time for you to quit screwing around. If you would add 30 pounds, you'd be a stud-hoss."

"Coach," Lee answered, "I'm that already."

The late Pat Watson was Bill Dooley's offensive coordinator and assistant head coach. Like Dooley, he was a no-nonsense Southern ball coach who was a star guard at Mississippi State. During one intense spring drill inside Rector Field House, an out-of-shape lineman fell in a heap on the turf.

"Son, are you all right?" Watson said.

"I don't know," the player groaned.

"Well, can you breathe?"

"Oh…oh… barely…"

"Can you get up?"

"Oooh, no, I …can't get up…"

"Well if you can't get up," Watson said, "then roll your fat [butt] off the carpet."

One afternoon Carter Wiley and Steve Johnson were hanging around the desk of Sharon McCloskey, then a football secretary, who was in the process of sorting recruiting questionnaires the football office had mailed to high school prospects. When she left her desk to make a copy, Wiley snagged a blank questionnaire, found an empty room and began filling it out for fun. Under height, they wrote, "6'-7"." Under weight, "350." They filled in a forty time of 4.4. The bench press was 450. At the end of the form, there was a question about the student's preferred field of study. They wrote,

"Engineering," adding, "I've always wanted to drive a train." They folded the bogus form and slipped it into McCloskey's stack.

The next day Coach Dooley called Wiley and Johnson into his office. "Well, hell, boys, you think this all is pretty funny," he said. "You caused a real scramble in this office yesterday. When we saw those numbers, we couldn't figure out how we let that kid slip by. Then we saw your little note at the bottom."

Wiley and Johnson looked at each other, then turned to Dooley. "How did you know it was us?" Wiley said.

"There was no return address," Dooley said, the tipoff that he had been an inside job. "That's when we figured it had to be you."

In 2001, former free safety Carter Wiley was on his tractor—the one with the air-conditioned cab and radio—mowing the grass at his farm at The Plains, listening to a West Virginia game on FM 97.5. It had been a tough game for the Mountaineers, and afterward, defensive coordinator Phil Elmassian was being interviewed. Wiley listened with interest, since Elmassian was his position coach at Tech from 1985-86. When Elmassian was done, Wiley grinned and just shook his head.

The following Monday he called Elmassian. "Hey Elmo, I heard you on the radio this weekend," he said. "Man, you got to get some new material. That was the same shit you told me 15 years ago."

Carter Wiley and Phil Elmassian always had a stormy relationship. Wiley considered attending Virginia, but according to the book *Hoos N' Hokies: 100 Years of Virginia/Virginia Tech Football*, he opted for Tech because Virginia wanted him to take a foreign language course.

He and Elmo would go at each other, and when Elmo would get mad, he'd say, "You're at the wrong school. You're too much of a [bleeping] peacock. You're too much of a prep. You should have gone to UVA."

After the 1986 season Bill Dooley and most of his staff were fired, and Elmassian took a job as a Virginia assistant. "Isn't this ironic, Coach?" Wiley said to Elmo. "Now YOU'RE the one who belongs at Virginia, not me."

A star tailback at W.T. Woodson High in Fairfax, Virginia, Sean Donnelly was highly recruited on a regional level, with offers from Tech, Maryland, Virginia, and North Carolina State. Cavaliers head coach George Welsh and Terrapins coach Bobby Ross made home visits, which, in the end, wasn't a good idea.

Welsh formerly coached at Navy, and Donnelly's father, Jack, worked for the navy. He was a big Welsh fan. "But when I met him," Donnelly said, "he had the personality of a mustard jar."

Ross was extremely polite and a very nice man. But at the time, one of Maryland's top targets was a star wide receiver named Norris Davis. Apparently, that prospect was foremost on Ross' mind, because when he visited the Donnelly household he kept calling Sean "Norris."

So that was one kid Ross wasn't gonna get.

Bill Dooley and assistants Billy Hite and Lou Tepper flew up to visit Donnelly on a small plane. "They came to my school, all of them wearing long overcoats," Donnelly said. "They all looked so impressive."

While he had extremely good times on his official visits to Maryland and Virginia, Donnelly left Blacksburg with a black eye—literally. His hosts had taken him to Radford, where the players got into a fight and someone punched him. The next morning he was having lunch with his parents and Dooley at the Red Lion Inn. "What happened to your eye?" Dooley asked him. "Yes, son, what happened?" his mother said, concerned.

Donnelly's father elbowed him in the ribs. "Don't say anything," he whispered.

During the visit, Dooley told Donnelly that he was the only running back Tech was recruiting. "When I got there in 1983," Donnelly said, "I was competing with 14 other tailbacks. But I WAS the only one from Fairfax."

Sean Donnelly was 17 years old when he first arrived on campus. His father was helping him move into the athletic dorm when they came across two huge bearded men moving a sofa into the elevator.

"Wow, look at the size of those two guys," Jack Donnelly said. "It's a good thing those guys aren't playing. They look like they could hurt you."

Welcome to Division I football: the two hulks were Hokie linemen Vincent Johnson and Billy Leeson.

Wingback David Everett was the co-winner of Tech's prestigious Frank Loria Award in 1987. Among his fellow Hokies, however, he will be forever remembered as the man who helped set up The Kick. With 11 seconds left in the 1986 Peach Bowl, North Carolina State led Tech 24-22. The Hokies had the ball at the State 39-yard line. Everett had beaten safety Brian Gay; quarterback Erik Chapman saw him open and threw. Gay grabbed Everett and was flagged for pass interference.

"That made me mad," Everett said, "Before the game, my sister told me she'd give me all of her Christmas money if I scored a touchdown in the Peach Bowl. When I saw the ball coming at me, all I could think about was that cash."

Instead, he settled for victory when Kinzer nailed the 40-yarder, giving the Hokies their first-ever bowl win.

Kicker Chris Kinzer.

Tech's locker room was set up in numerical order, and tailback Eddie Hunter, one of the Hokies' big-play men, wore No. 45. Everett wore No. 46. "All season long, the media would gather around Eddie after the game, crowding me out," Everett said. "I'd lean over and tell them, 'If you need a really good quote, I'm available!' But they usually ignored me.

"They didn't ignore me that day, though."

Bill Dooley used to tape his weekly football show with host Jeff Charles on Saturday nights. This wasn't so bad for 1 p.m. home games; they would generally be done at four, giving Dooley and his wife, Marie, time to relax and have dinner with his staff at the Red Lion Inn from about seven till nine. At about 9:15 Charles would find Dooley and say, "Coach, we should be heading over to do the show," which they filmed on campus. The taping of the 30-minute program would usually take about an hour and a half, if everything went smoothly. "It could have been worse, but Coach Dooley really enjoyed doing that show," Charles said. "It was a big deal to him." They would have fun with it, inviting their wives along as sort of a studio audience.

The tough days came following road games, especially night road games. "Those were awful," Charles said. "We would literally get finished taping the show at three or four in the morning." Those were the nights the wives elected not to hang around.

It was after the road game at Virginia in 1985 that Dooley unsuccessfully tried to stifle a sneeze. If it had been a home day game, the producers would have screamed, "Cut!" But in the wee hours of the morning, all he got was a "Bless you!"

CHAPTER FIVE

Beamerball

With each passing year, Frank Beamer's aura continues to grow. He has taken Virginia Tech to the national championship game. Bowl trips are part of the annual budget. He has his own web site (Beamerball.com) and restaurant (Beamer's). He's won almost every individual coaching honor. All that's left to seal his legendary status is a BCS Championship ring.

But while Beamer runs things on the field, it is Dr. John Ballein who takes care of everything else. "I don't think Coach Beamer could operate with Ballein," said former star defensive end Corey Moore.

Ballein, Tech's associate director of athletics for football operations, is a Great American Success Story. A linebacker at Indiana (Pennsylvania), he graduated with a degree in physical education and health in 1983. In 1987, he was trying to hook up with a Division I-A school and sent out 100 videotapes extolling his virtues. "I didn't know anybody," he said, "so I had to make myself different."

He was different, all right: the video featured a picture of Ballein from his playing days, wearing a mohawk haircut.

Florida head coach Ron Zook, then a Tech assistant, got a copy of the tape and appreciated Ballein's gumption. He showed it to assistant coach Billy Hite.

"What do you think, Billy?" Zook said when it was done.

51

Decorum prohibits us from repeating Hite's exact words, but to paraphrase, he questioned Ballein's [bleeping] sexual preference.

Zook then showed the tape to Beamer, who figured Ballein was a few clowns shy of a circus.

"I'm not too sure about this guy," were his exact words.

But Zook convinced Beamer to give Ballein a chance, and he came aboard as a graduate assistant. After a brief stint at Western Kentucky, Ballein returned as Tech's recruiting coordinator. Since then, his rise has matched that of the Hokies'.

"I'm a pretty good judge of character," Beamer said, "but I was wrong that time. This place wouldn't run without John Ballein."

Don't just write off that comment as Frank Beamer, a people-oriented guy, being loyal to one of his staff members. Ballein has been crucial to Tech's success, and outside parties have taken note. According to Nike Football Training Camp executive director Andy Bark, "Tech's football operations guy, John Ballein, is the best in the country. ... If all of Coach Beamer's staff is like this guy, it's easy to see why Tech is a top 10 football program."

Ballein's efficiency and his uncanny ability to cover every little detail when it comes to bowl preparation didn't go unnoticed by Gary Cavalli, executive director of the San Francisco Bowl. "We've been in regular contact with Mr. John Ballein," Cavalli said during a bowl teleconference. "He is Mr. Organization, I tell you. I thought the Air Force guys were tight, but [Ballein] has it buttoned down to a science."

October 4, 1997, was not the best of days for offensive line coach J.B. Grimes. Miami of Ohio upset the Hokies in Blacksburg 24-17, and that morning Grimes experienced chest pains.

Before the game he went to the hospital, where he was examined and released. But as he stood on the sideline before the

Dr. John Ballein.

game, he still wasn't feeling well. Beamer took one look at him and told him to go up to the coach's press box and sit down.

It was a tense game and John Ballein was watching a play through his binoculars. He turned around to find a white-faced Grimes splayed out the floor, holding his chest.

"I think ... I'm hurtin'..." he gasped. "I think ... you better get me ... a doctor ..."

"OK," Ballein said, "just as soon as this series is over."

Frank Beamer has won almost every national coaching award there is, and nobody has more loyalty from his assistants. That's because Beamer treats them so well. "He's the Cajun cook," said quarterbacks coach Kevin Rogers, who has been at Syracuse and Notre Dame. "He has his own recipe. This is the first place I've ever been where I was free to work out during lunchtime."

Richmond Times-Dispatch writer Mike Harris said he was leaving the Merryman Center one day when he spotted Rogers sitting on the concrete ledge outside. He stopped and chatted informally about how Rogers was adjusting to life in Blacksburg. "You know," he said, "if I was at Syracuse or Notre Dame, I wouldn't be sitting here talking to you now."

Rogers related to Harris one of his first conversations with Beamer. "What is your policy toward the media?" he had asked him. "What are you talking about?" Beamer replied. "Our policy is, if they ask you a question, you answer it."

"Gee, that's great," Rogers said.

Said Harris, "The stuff that worries many coaches doesn't bother Beamer."

The coach always seems to be in control even when things aren't going well. In 2001 the Hokies were upset at home against Syracuse. After the game, Beamer complained that the Orangemen's kicker brought a butterscotch Dum-Dum on the field to help line up his kick. It's like the old golf trick, he said, and it's illegal. The following Tuesday, *Roanoke Times* sportswriter Randy King stopped at a Christiansburg convenience store and purchased a cherry Charm's Super Blow Pop and set it on Beamer's chair.

"Man, I don't know about that," *Richmond Times-Dispatch* writer Mike Harris told King. "Beamer wasn't real happy about that loss. I don't know if it's a good idea."

"Aw, hell, he'll be all right," King said.

Harris shrugged and waited for the explosion. Beamer arrived, pulled out his chair, saw the lollipop and stared at it for a moment. Then he laughed and pointed at King. "If you turned that thing and put it on the ground," he said, "and you're trying to hit that golf ball straight …"

Later that day, Tech placekicker Carter Warley was asked if a butterscotch Dum-Dum would help him line up a kick. "I don't see where a lollipop would help me," he said. "I would need a big old road sign pointing toward the goal posts that say, 'THIS way.'"

Frank Beamer has a web site called Beamerball.com. Although fans love it, the site has been a sticky subject with writers, because the site often breaks inside scoops before releasing them to the media.

During one press conference, a writer asked Beamer, "What's up with DeAngelo Hall moving from cornerback to rover?"

"That's not true," Beamer said. "Where did you get that from?"

"Your web site," the writer said.

"Hold on, I'll be right back."

Beamer left and returned two minutes later.

"That's been fixed," he said. "It was a typo."

Although Frank Beamer is the consummate southern gentleman off the field, during games he is an intense competitor. *Richmond Times-Dispatch* writer Mike Harris was at practice one day when deep snapper Travis Conway was having a bad day. Beamer, who coaches the special teams, went nuts. He screamed at Conway, "This next snap is the most important snap of your collegiate career."

Conway then drilled a beautiful bullet—"the most perfect snap in the history of college football," according to Harris—which punter Vinnie Burns promptly dropped.

"For the next five minutes," Harris said, "I was witness to the most non-Frank Beamer behavior I have ever seen."

Official Tom Beck got a load of the Beamer temper out one afternoon after making a call that went against the Hokies. "You [bleeper-bleeper]!" Beamer screamed at Beck. "You blew that call, you [bleeper-bleeper]!"

A few games later that same season, Beck was working another Virginia Tech game. Beamer and assistant coach Billy Hite met with the officials before kickoff. "Coach," Hite said, "You remember Tom Beck."

Beamer looked at him blankly.

Beck nodded and pointed to himself. "[Bleeper-bleeper]," he said.

"Oh, right," Beamer nodded.

A few games later, Beck was working the Hokies once again. Before the game, he approached Coach Beamer, who by now recognized him on sight. "Now listen, Coach," Beck said, "I'm going to be on the opposite sideline today. So if you disagree with a call, you're going to have to yell pretty loud, and I'd appreciate it if you'd address me as MISTER [bleeper-bleeper]."

The postgame interviews for the road team at Miami's Orange Bowl take place under metal bleachers. "You've got spilled drinks dripping through the cracks and peanut shells falling on your shoulders," said *Richmond Times-Dispatch* sportswriter Mike Harris. "And it is nearly impossible to hear what the coach is saying because people are stomping around up above."

Defensive back Loren Johnson.

After the Hokies' 2000 game in Miami, a Hurricane fan stuck his head through the bleachers and yelled to Beamer in a rant that included the word [butt]hole.

"Well," Beamer said as he addressed the reporters, "he got one word right."

Friday before a home football game, cornerback John Granby couldn't find his workout shirt and asked equipment manager Lester Karlin for a new one. Karlin gave him the obligatory cursing out and fetched him a new shirt. He was getting ready to fling it at Granby when the player grabbed the shirt and yanked it toward him— popping Karlin's arm from its socket.

Luckily, trainer Eddie Ferrell was in the training room next door.

When Eddie Ferrell died in 1998, it rocked the Hokie football community. Players wore "EF" decals on their helmets in his honor, and the athletics department established a memorial scholarship fund in his honor.

Ferrell earned his undergraduate degree at Arkansas, where his father was a longtime trainer. He followed in his footsteps, working for two seasons as an assistant trainer with the Minnesota Vikings and for two seasons at Oregon State. He returned to Arkansas as an assistant trainer under Frank Broyles in 1970.

He came to Tech in 1971 when Charlie Coffey was named the Hokies' head football coach. Ferrell and Coffey had worked together at Arkansas. During the Coffey years, the Jimmy Sharpe years, the Bill Dooley years and the Beamer years, Ferrell was a constant, always taking care of his beloved players and tweaking everybody with his quick wit.

In 1987, Beamer struggled through a difficult 2-9 inaugural season, where the offense was particularly anemic. That season there was a tragedy where a student fell from the east stands.

"You didn't hear about it?" Ferrell asked Beamer.

"No, what happened?"

"You finally got a first down and a student was so surprised, she passed out from shock and fell right out of Lane Stadium."

It was a Friday afternoon, and the Hokies flew to Boston to play the Eagles. After the workout, each player was supposed to have an individual box of Kentucky Fried Chicken waiting for him.

On the bus ride from Logan airport to Alumni Stadium, John Ballein asked trainer Eddie Ferrell, "Hey, did you remember to call the chicken guy?"

"Yeah, yeah," Ferrell said. "Give me your [cell] phone."

Ferrell walked to the back of the bus and called the KFC to check on the status of his chicken. The person on the other line didn't know what he was talking about.

"I talked to the manager this morning!" a panicked Ferrell said. "We need 120 boxes of chicken delivered in an hour!"

After some haggling, the person agreed to take the order. From the front of the bus, Ballein heard Ferrell scream in a high-pitched voice, "I don't care! I don't care! Just get cookin'!"

Ferrell returned to his seat. "You order the chicken?" said Ballein, trying to keep a straight face. He had heard every word.

"Yeah," Ferrell said. "It's not ready yet."

"Really?" Ballein said. "So what is it that you don't care about?"

"The idiots asked me if I wanted Original or Extra Crispy."

On Saturday morning the Hokies stood outside the Fairmont (West Virginia) Holiday Inn, waiting for the buses to take them to Mountaineer Field. But when they arrived, there were only two buses when there were supposed to be four. The other two were stuck in traffic.

Ferrell fell into a panic.

"It's OK, Eddie," Ballein said. "We'll load the players and coaches into the two buses. Everybody else can wait." As they were doing that he third bus arrived, which took the support staff.

Ballein and Ferrell waited for the last bus.

It rolled up and they jumped on. "You know, if we hurry," Ballein told the driver, "We can catch the other buses and get the police escort."

Ferrell loved that idea. "Yeah, we gotta GO!" he said.

As they ramped onto I-79, Ballein elbowed Ferrell. "Hey Eddie, look, sitting in front of the hotel!" he said. "There's your briefcase!"

When the hotel shipped it back to Blacksburg, Ferrell opened it to find he had packed the TV remote control from his room.

After so many misadventures, some in the Hokies' camp suspected Ferrell had attention deficit disorder. Administrator Sharon McCloskey asked him about it.

"Yeah, I think I do have ADD," he said. "I'm going to take a class to help me with it."

Next week McCloskey asked Ferrell how the class went.

"I don't know," he said. "I forgot where it was."

In the August of 1991, Tech's highly touted secondary of Tyronne Drakeford, Greg Lassiter, Damien Russell and John Granby was searching for a nickname. They opted for "The Dark Zone," because, as Russell put it, "you step into the Dark Zone, and it's lights out."

Things didn't go quite as they had planned that season, and the Hokies stumbled to a 5-6 record. The Dark Zone became known as that section of the field you pass through before entering the end zone.

In 1992, the athletics department was financially strapped and had to find creative ways to save money. Tech's first road game of the year was at East Carolina, and the team waited on the Roanoke Regional Airport tarmac for the charter plane, delayed because of mechanical difficulties.

Coach Frank Beamer, suspecting one source of the department's frugality, turned to assistant athletics director Jeff Bourne. "Do you feel good about this plane deal?" he said.

"I feel good about this deal," Bourne said.

Just then everybody looked up. "There it is!" a player said.

Descending was a plane painted a garish shade of lime green.

"Hey!" said another player. "It looks like a giant pickle!"

Bourne's face turned bright red.

The team piled into the Boeing 727 and waited. In the seat-back pockets were safety instructions for "Air Guadalupe." Outside the temperature was 90 degrees, and everybody began to sweat. Finally the pilot came on the intercom and said there were further mechanical problems, but that they always keep a maintenance worker as part of the crew.

Assistant John Ballein turned to Beamer. "They kept a maintenance worker on board?"

On cue, a short fellow in overalls named Jose ran down the aisle, carrying nothing but a screwdriver.

"He's going to fix this big plane with that?" Beamer said.

Everybody waited for what seemed like an eternity.

"I'd feel a whole lot better if he had a bigger screwdriver," said graduate assistant James Brown.

Jose was trying to open the starter valve on the No. 3 engine, and Ballein went to check on his progress.

"Coach, I've got good news and bad news," Ballein said upon his return.

"Give me the good news first," Beamer said.

"The good news is, Jose said the plane is fixed and we're ready to take off."

"That's great! What's the bad news?"

"Jose is standing on the tarmac waving goodbye."

It was very late one Saturday night when the Virginia Tech team returned from an evening game at South Carolina in 1989. The Hokies' chartered USAir plane had to circle the Roanoke airport for 30 minutes because the airport had turned off its runway lights.

"As soon as we can find someone down there to turn on the lights, we can land," said the pilot.

Few would disagree that Beamer is Virginia Tech's all-time greatest coach, but in 1992, when his team struggled to a disappointing 2-8-1 mark, a certain percentage of Hokie fans wanted him fired.

After that season, Beamer spoke at a Hokie Club function in Wytheville, Virginia. He sat down to eat with a group of alumni and his host introduced him to a man named John Beamer.

"John Beamer," the coach repeated. "You know, I grew up right over that mountain, in Hillsville. We could be related."

He said, "Not this year, we're not."

Oh yeah, 1992 was a rough season all right. After another tough loss, Frank Beamer and his wife, Cheryl, boarded a small university plane so he could return in time to film his television

Coach Frank Beamer.

show. According to the *Roanoke Times,* Cheryl was taking the loss a little harder than her husband, so he tried to make her feel better.

"Cheryl," he said, "I'm going to take this $100 bill and throw it out the window to make someone down there happy."

Her eyes lit up. "You know what?" she said. "I'm going to take two $100 bills and throw them out the window and make two people happy."

From the cockpit, the pilot yelled back, "Coach, why don't you jump out that window and make everybody happy?"

Virginia Tech had a breakthrough season in 1993, going 9-3 and beating Indiana in the Independence Bowl. But everybody would like to forget the 48-34 loss at Boston College that year, when quarterback Glenn Foley was 21 of 29 for 448 yards.

The Eagles had run four plays—all for big yardage—when Hokies defensive coordinator Phil Elmassian growled, "We can't stop them," and threw off his headset.

Beamer looked at the scoreboard. Only a few minutes had ticked off the clock.

"This is not good," he said.

Guard William Boatwright was one of five Hokies taken in the 1992 NFL draft. Philadelphia chose him in the seventh round. "The first thing that went through my mind was, 'Hey, I got drafted,'" he said. "The second thing was, 'Oh, great, in practice, I'm going to have to block Reggie White.'"

Chicago took quarterback Will Furrer in the fourth round. He left almost immediately to participate in the Bears' mini-camp. "One of my biggest problems," he said before leaving, "will be figuring out whether to call Mike Singletary 'Mister' or 'Sir.'"

One of the key recruiting coups in the Frank Beamer era was the 1993 signing of defensive end Cornell Brown out of E.C. Glass High School in Lynchburg, Virginia. The Hokies were coming off a disappointing 2-8-1 season, and Brown was ranked among the top five players in the state. At that time, Tech rarely signed a player of his caliber, and his signing was a big part of the program's turnaround.

Brown had narrowed his choices to Tech and Virginia, and he called a press conference at his high school to announce his decision. He leaned toward the mic and said, "I'm going to the University of Virginia…"

And before the Tech fans could let out a groan, he added, "Tech."

Defensive end Cornell Brown.

Later, Hokies assistant John Ballein went up to Brown. "Why did you do that?" he said. "Were you trying to have some fun with us, or what?"

Brown shook his head. "At the time," he said, "that was what I thought the school was called."

On signing day 1995, Tech inked 16 players, 11 from Virginia, but just two made the *Roanoke Times* Top 25 list (offensive lineman Keith Short and defensive back Tyron Edmond). Only a handful from that class made notable contributions—Short, defensive end Chris Cyrus, linebacker Michael Hawkes, defensive back Loren Johnson, linebacker Jamel Smith and lineman Nathaniel Williams. After back-to-back bowl games, one might expect a better class, but in late March it got a huge boost when some scholarships opened up. Among those late signees were wide receiver Ricky Hall and defensive backs Pierson Prioleau and Keion Carpenter. Hall was a starting wide receiver for the Hokies' 1999 team that finished ranked No. 2 in the nation, while Prioleau and Carpenter are in the NFL.

Before Virginia Tech's 1993 home game with Bowling Green, a case of measles descended upon campus and people feared that it could spread. A local TV station contacted Tech sports information director Jack Williams.

"This is really a university matter, not an athletics matter," Williams told the reporter, and referred him to Tech's administrative building. "You really should get a statement from Burruss Hall."

"Fine, Jack," said the reporter. "Can you give me his number?"

Tech's 1995 game at Rutgers was played on a rainy October afternoon. At kickoff, water had pooled up on the sideline. Maybe all the subliminal messaging was too much for one defensive player; in the huddle, he turned to tackle J.C. Price.

"J.C.," he grimaced, "I really have to use the bathroom."

"Shoot, man, look around," Price said. "It's raining like hell and you're covered in mud. Just let it go. Nobody will know."

The player nodded.

"Feel better?" Price asked a moment later.

"A little," he said, "but it's awfully warm."

The Hokies had plane trouble following their 26-16 win over Pittsburgh in 1995. The team found a large room at the Sheraton to wait while a new plane arrived. While the rest of the team watched the Notre Dame-Ohio State game, the seniors got pizzas. Offensive tackle Jay Hagood took the cheese and sausage off a huge slice of pizza and dropped it into his mouth.

"Is there anything wrong with the crust?" a staff member asked him.

"No," he shrugged.

Defensive tackle J.C. Price was straight out of a 1960s-era NFL Films reel: mud caked on his face, a clod of sod stuck in the crack of his facemask, an oversized cast on his left forearm. He was a big (6'3", 285) pigeon-toed throwback with a linebacker's speed.

His high school nickname was "Ogre" and he showed up on campus with a scruffy goatee and wild hair. Coach Frank Beamer took one look at him and turned to Billy Hite, who had recruited Price. "That kid better be a player," he said.

During his freshman year, Price's typical day went like this: he rose at noon, ate, played Sega, went to practice, came home, played

Sega and drank beer, stayed up till six in the morning, went to sleep, and then started the routine all over again.

He finished his first semester with three Fs and a D. According to the *Roanoke Times,* Price's parents taped his report card to the family TV during the Christmas holidays for everybody to see. "It was awfully humbling," he said.

Price began to turn things around, and by his junior year he had earned a 2.9 grade point average. The Carolina Panthers took him in the third round of the 1996 NFL draft. A back injury kept him from playing professionally. He kept trying to rehab his back and signed a free agent contract with Chicago in 1998.

"I started failing physicals," he told the *Roanoke Times.* "I failed one with the Bears and I failed one with the World League. When you're an All-Pro and failing physicals, that's one thing. But when you're aspiring just to be a quality backup and fail a physical, your career is pretty much over."

Now, the class-skipping freshman is earning his master's degree and working as a graduate assistant.

"The GA post doesn't pay anything, really," he said. "Basically, it's like being on scholarship again. They pay for my grad school."

It was the Friday night before Tech's 1995 game at West Virginia. *Richmond Times-Dispatch* writers John Markon and Skip Wood were hanging out at the hotel. It was around 9 p.m., and coach Frank Beamer came walking through the lobby. He stopped to say hello, and the three went into the lounge for a drink. Wood was amazed.

"Coach, you've got a big game tomorrow," he said. "Shouldn't you be watching film or something?"

"Skip," Beamer said, "the hay is in the barn."

Indeed it was. The Hokies beat the Mountaineers 27-0.

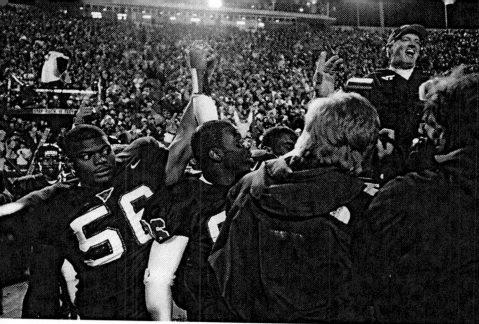

Frank Beamer and team celebrate their win over Boston College.

Virginia Tech clinched its first Big East championship on November 11, 1995 with a 38-16 win over Temple in Washington's RFK Stadium. Hokie fans rained the field with oranges and sugar cubes. Somebody even threw a pool ball onto the field, even though there was no Billiards Bowl.

Thankfully for those on the sidelines, no reptiles were tossed. The Gator Bowl was not an option.

The Hokie football team was in a jocular mood on the flight home. Before takeoff a flight attendant worked her way down the aisle, doing a safety check. "Seatbelt?" she asked senior Rich Bowen.

"No, thank you," he said. "I already have one."

The team experienced turbulence on the flight, putting a scare into everybody. On the bouncy approach to Roanoke Regional Airport, the pilot came on the intercom and said the plane would land in five to ten minutes.

"Yeah," said offensive tackle Jay Hagood, "one way or another."

At the 1995 Sugar Bowl, center Keith Short broke curfew—not only that, he stiffed the cabbie who took him back to the hotel. The next morning John Ballein paid for a Greyhound bus ticket back to Blacksburg—a most unpleasant 23-hour ride. Today, however, Short said that was one of the best things that ever happened to him. When the bus reached the Tennessee mountains, he realized he had to do something with his life.

In 1998, the Hokies were bussing back to Blacksburg from a rousing 38-8 win over Alabama in the Music City Bowl. Said a happy Short: "I never thought I'd want to see those Tennessee mountains from a bus again."

A huge, beat-up black lunch pail, with a crudely painted "VT" on its side, hangs from the ceiling of the Merryman Center Hall of Legends. It represents the Hokies' blue-collar work ethic. The pail originated during the 1995 season, when Tech co-defensive coordinator Rod Sharpless found it. Actually, it was his mother-in-law, who lived in Mercerville, N.J. The pail had belonged to a coal miner.

"It's a symbol of our defense," said co-defensive coordinator Bud Foster. "We're blue-collar guys who bring their lunch to work every day."

Tech's top defensive player of the week takes responsibility for the pail, which goes with the team to practice, team meetings, the bus, the plane, the hotel.

OK, the pail's symbolism, we get that. But two defensive coordinators? That is sooo '90s.

After the Hokies won the Sugar Bowl, J.C. Price didn't parade around the field with the Sugar Bowl trophy; he held that beat-up old lunch pail up in one hand, shaking his fist with the other. *Roanoke Times* columnist Jack Bogaczyk wrote, "And the lunch pail? It should be retired. It should sit in a trophy case when Tech's new $6 million football facility is completed, right next to the Sugar

The lunch pail represents the Hokies' blue-collar work ethic.

Bowl [trophy]. One belongs with the other. They wouldn't have gotten one without the other."

At the end of the game, you could hear the chant: "First quarter, second quarter, third quarter, fourth quarter, French Quarter."

Before the 1999 season, Frank Beamer said his club's goal wasn't to go 11-0 during the regular season.

The goal was to go 1-0.

Eleven times.

The No. 2 Hokies pulled it off on a post-Thanksgiving Friday evening—funny, as time goes by, it seemed like a Saturday—with a 38-14 win over No. 22 Boston College. The stage was set to face No. 1 Florida State in the Sugar Bowl, as long as the computers didn't spring No. 3 Nebraska past the Hokies. And the Cornhuskers were in the process of pummeling Colorado.

While Michael Vick was working his magic against the Eagles, the Lane Stadium PA announcer kept fans abreast of the Big 12 showdown. Hokie fans cheered when the Buffaloes mounted a comeback. They missed a 34-yard field goal with one second left, drawing a groan from the Lane faithful.

In the fourth quarter, the PA announcer proclaimed a Colorado victory, drawing wild cheers. But the report was wrong: the Huskers scored a touchdown on their overtime possession, winning 33-30.

As the final seconds ticked off in Blacksburg, the scene was surreal. The game was over, but nobody left. Queen's "We Are the Champions" blared over the loudspeakers. Little white sugar cubes rained down on the field like hail. Students jumped from the retaining walls to the field, swarming players and attacking the north goal post. Others got down on their knees and grabbed a handful of souvenir sod.

Amid all this, Beamer stood on a makeshift platform at midfield, microphone in hand, asking, "How many of y'all am I gonna see in New Orleans?"

The crowd roared, but deep down, they worried, "Would Nebraska pass us in the BCS computer rankings?"

The most exciting game in Virginia Tech's undefeated 1999 regular season came on November 6 at Morgantown against a 3-5 West Virginia team. Prior to kickoff, Minnesota upset No. 2 Penn State. If the Hokies could beat the Mountaineers, they would take the Nittany Lions' place in the rankings.

Tech led 19-7 with 4:59 to play thanks to a 51-yard pass from Michael Vick to Andre Davis that set up a six-yard Shyrone Stith scoring run. Things looked very good when WVU's Richard Bryant fumbled the ensuing kickoff. But the ball bounced right into the hands of Boo Sensabaugh, who returned it 44 yards to the Hokies' 39. Punter Jimmy Kibble hit him out of bounds, tacking on another 15 yards, and suddenly the Mountaineers had the ball at the Tech 24. They scored four plays later, making it 19-14 with 3:15 left.

Scary, but no time for Tech fans to panic.

The Hokies smartly tried to run as much clock as they could. Stith was up to the assignment, getting good yardage, but the Mountaineers finally figured out what was going on. All-Big East linebacker Barrett Green keyed on Stith and knocked the ball loose. Sensabaugh recovered again and WVU scored four plays later. Suddenly the Mountaineers led 20-19 with 1:15 left.

Now it was time for Tech fans to panic.

Lucky for them, Vick was calm. While the Mountaineers were going in for the score, offensive coordinator Rickey Bustle kept talking to Vick through the headphones. He didn't want Vick to get caught up in watching the game and getting disappointed if WVU scored. They discussed the two-minute drill and what plays might work best. He said to assume the Mountaineers would score. One of the last things he told Vick was, "Don't forget, you can always pull it down and run."

As West Virginia prepared to kick off, Tech defensive ends Corey Moore and John Engelberger handicapped their chances, according to the *Daily Press*. "If [Vick] is as good as advertised," Moore said, "he'll make something happen."

In the huddle, Vick told his teammates, "We're gonna drive down the field and win this game. All we need is a field goal."

According to David Teel's (Newport News) *Daily Press* story, on first down, Vick lined up in the shotgun with two receivers spread to each side. In studying West Virginia's prevent on tape, Tech coaches noticed the safeties backpedaling quickly into deep zone coverage. Ricky Hall, crossing from right to left, was going to be open 15-20 yards downfield.

But this time the safeties didn't drop; Hall was covered. Vick read the change and saw Andre Davis open underneath on a short yard crossing pattern. Vick's pass into the left flat was high and behind Davis, incomplete, setting up second and 10 with 1:06 left.

"Oh, man," Vick thought. "I've got to get us something on this play."

In the huddle, Vick called a play both he and Bustle liked—a sprint out to the right with Terrell Parham the primary receiver running a quick sideline pattern. Against soft zone coverage, Vick hit Parham for 14 yards to the 29. The first down stopped the clock with 1:01 left.

According to Teel's story, Vick wanted more and called for a sprint-out to the left with Parham and Davis running deep routes. The play had never worked during Tech's weekly hurry-up drills. Upstairs, Bustle grimaced at the call, and just as he expected, West Virginia blanketed Davis and Parham. Vick found a secondary receiver, Hall, for a nine-yard gain to the 38. He didn't get out of bounds, and as the Hokies scrambled to line up the clock ticked down: 50 seconds, 40 seconds.

The next play was the same call as the one on first down: Vick looking for Hall on a midrange crossing route. Again, West Virginia's safeties clogged the passing lanes, but this time Vick rolled to his right. He outraced linebacker Shannon Washington and tackle Greg Robinette to the corner, and at the 34-yard line raised his left arm to throw. Then he remembered what Bustle had told him on the sideline. He ran. Nine yards downfield, at Tech's 45, he encountered Green, who tried to force Vick out of bounds.

That's when Vick went into another gear, zoomed past Green, hurdled defensive back Perlo Bastien and went out of bounds at the West Virginia 36.

"I don't know how fast he was going," said Frank Beamer, "but if we'd have had a stopwatch, it would have been the fastest 40-yard dash he has ever run."

The Hokies still needed a few more yards; a 53-yarder might have been pushing it for placekicker Shayne Graham. But this was no time to get greedy.

The play was for all four receivers to run hook routes. Vick found Hall for nine yards to the 27. Vick, excited, thought to himself, "I did it! I did it!" He was jumping around, going crazy, trying to get everybody lined up. He spiked the ball with five seconds left.

WVU called timeout to ice Graham as he set up for the 44-yard attempt. On the sideline, the Tech players were on their knees, holding hands. Some couldn't bear to watch.

Holder Caleb Hurd told Teel that the timeout actually helped them. "It took our nerves away," he said. "We had a chance to catch our breath."

At 7:20 p.m. Eastern time, Cliff Anders' snap was perfect and Graham nailed it. The Hokies won 22-20.

To this day people still ask Beamer what he said before Graham attempted his kick.

Beamer always answers it the same way. "I'll tell you what I said. I said a prayer."

One season a flu epidemic hit 42 Hokie players. Coach Frank Beamer was meeting with one of the players, who had failed a summer school class.

"I was really hacked off," Beamer told the *Roanoke Times*. "I usually don't get too mad, but I was really upset over this. I said, 'So and so, you really made me mad.' I really tore into him pretty good. I went on and on about it for a few minutes and he never said a word."

After chewing out the kid, Beamer sat back in his chair. About a minute went by and the two sat there in silence.

"Coach," the player finally said, "you don't have that bug, too, do you?"

During his freshman year, the sports information department asked defensive end John Engelberger to appear at the weekly Tuesday press luncheon. "Hey, great, free food," he thought. But when he arrived, he saw TV cameras set up on the patio. His eyes got big and he began to sweat.

"I've got to talk to them?" he asked sports information director Dave Smith.

"Well, yes, that's part of it," Smith said, but he could tell Engelberger was uncomfortable. So he let him eat lunch and sent him home.

Engelberger wasn't bashful, but he hated to talk to the media. "He would joke with you," Jimmy Robertson, editor of *Hokie Sports The Newspaper*. "But as soon as you pulled out a pen and paper, he wouldn't say a thing."

He learned to overcome that to a certain extent. During his senior year, *ESPN* and *Sports Illustrated* were on campus, and Engelberger went up to John Ballein. "Which reporter is from *SI*?" he said.

Ballein pointed to him, and Engelberger strolled over.

"Hello, who are you with?" he said, "the *Blacksburg Sentinel*?"

During the 1999 season, Tech was coming home after a 58-20 win at Rutgers. The return trip turned into a nightmare. On the way to the airport, the bus broke down. Then the plane couldn't land in Roanoke because of bad weather. The team flew to Greensboro, where it waited for the buses to arrive. Just south of Roanoke, one of those buses broke down at around 5 a.m.

Everybody was tired, hungry and cranky. "I'm going to beat up the bus driver and get arrested," Engelberger said. "At least in jail, I'll have a meal and a warm bed to sleep in."

When he signed his first NFL contract with the 49ers, Engelberger said the first thing he was going to do was visit the junkyard down from his house in northern Virginia and buy a hubcap for his 1992 burgundy Chevy Lumina.

When San Francisco reacquired defensive lineman Dana Stubblefield, John Engelberger didn't mind giving up his No. 95— but he wanted to keep his locker.

"I'll give you $1,000 for it," Stubblefield said.

Engelberger said no.

"Two thousand," Stubblefield said.

"Naw."

"Six thousand."

"Listen," Engelberger said, "how about you just buy me two cases of Budweiser."

The next day, a beer truck pulled up to Engelberger's apartment and the driver unloaded two cases, including a note from the distributor.

"Thanks for your loyalty to our product," read the note. "If you need anything else, please let us know."

Knowing Engelberger, he was probably thinking, "Leave the truck."

When quarterbacks coach Kevin Rogers joined the Tech staff for the 2002 season, he knew he was going to hear about his tenure at league rival Syracuse. Before becoming the offensive coordinator at Notre Dame, Rogers had been with the Orangemen from 1991-98 and had mentored Donovan McNabb.

Ah, McNabb.

Tech's 1998 game at the Carrier Dome was one of the wildest, craziest, most exciting games it has ever played—and one of its most excruciating losses.

"I've never been in a game that had such divided perspectives," Rogers said. "When I came here, everybody was telling me how devastated they were, how Tech should have won that game. But at Syracuse, everybody believed they should have won the game."

The statistics back up Rogers. No. 25 Syracuse out-gained No. 12 Tech by a whopping 440 yards to 152. It controlled the ball for 37 minutes to Tech's 23. The Hokies had scored on several fluke plays, including a 74-yard fumble return for a score. Defensive back Keion Carpenter had popped the ball free from the ball carrier, and it squirted in the air; defensive back Loren Johnson caught it in full stride. Wrote Will Stewart of Tech Sideline.com: "The Carrier Dome fell so quiet, I could hear a guy in the top row chewing a pretzel. A soft pretzel."

The game went back and forth, and with 4:52 to play, the Hokies, who still had hopes of a BCS bid, led 26-22. Syracuse faced a fourth and seven, but McNabb burst up the middle on a draw for 41 yards. With 0:51 left, the Orangemen had first and goal. Tech stuffed them on first down; then defensive end Corey Moore burst through the line to sack McNabb at the 13. He hastily lined his team up and spiked the ball with five seconds to go. Time for one more play.

Tech called timeout to the chagrin of some fans. McNabb had just vomited on the field and appeared exhausted; the TO gave him time to collect himself. But defensive coordinator Bud Foster knew what play McNabb was going to run next, and he wanted to have his defense ready.

"Oh, we were going to run Donovan out to the right and throw back across the field to the tight end," Rogers said. "That was kind of his signature play. Bud knew that."

But didn't the timeout give him a needed break, after blowing grits on the field?

"This was Donovan McNabb. It wouldn't have mattered."

What happened next is what makes college football so great, and sometimes so maddening. Even though they knew it was coming, the Hokies had a breakdown in coverage, and tight end Stephen Brominski did a great job of positioning. McNabb's signature play was a success, and Syracuse won 28-26.

Ernest Wilford set the Virginia Tech single-season record for receptions in 2002 and set a Big East record with 279 receiving yards, against Syracuse. But before that, he was remembered as The Guy Who Dropped The Pass.

In 2001, Tech hosted No. 1 Miami and trailed 20-3 at halftime. It mounted a furious second-half rally, and when Brandon Manning ran in a blocked punt from 22 yards out, the score was 26-24 Miami with 6:03 to play. The crowd went berserk; Lane Stadium was as loud as it has ever been.

The Hokies lined up for the two-point conversion, and quarterback Grant Noel, who suffered through a horrendous game, found Wilford open and delivered a perfect pass. Wilford let the potential game-tying score slip through his arms. The Hurricanes held on to beat the Hokies. Miami went on to win the national title.

"I was hurt in the beginning, real hurt," Wilford told the *The Washington Post.* "Embarrassed. I felt like I let my team down. Afterward, I didn't want to talk to anyone for, like, three to four days. Didn't talk to my parents, didn't talk to anyone. I just wanted to be by myself and get myself straight. But I came to the conclusion I just had to use that game as motivation to get better."

The following April, director Spike Lee spoke on campus and bantered with the crowd of about 2,000. He brought up the Miami game. "Is the guy who dropped that pass here?" Lee asked. Wilford stood up, and, according to the *Post*, "threw his hands to the side of his head and pointed his palms outward to honor his fraternity, Omega Psi Phi, and barked loudly as is their tradition. He also stared Lee dead in the eyes."

Lee told Wilford, "Man, you messed up the whole bowl thing." Wilford laughed it off, but several students stuck up for him during a question-and-answer session. After the show, Lee apologized to Wilford.

The following summer, during August two-a-days, a nasty flu bug was going around the team. Wilford was the last one to come down with it.

"Well, what do you know," equipment manager Lester Karlin said. "Ernest Wilford finally caught something."

When you're in the Hokies' locker room, you've got to stay on your toes—sometimes quite literally. According to defensive back Aaron Rouse, one of cornerback/wide receiver DeAngelo Hall's favorite pranks is to cover a teammate's dressing stool with Icy Hot balm while he's in the shower. When he comes and sits down, he doesn't sit for long.

CHAPTER SIX

Michael Vick

I n a span of 17 years, Virginia Tech was blessed to have had two players taken No. 1 overall in the NFL draft: Bruce Smith and Michael Vick. What's amazing is that Vick established his legacy in the equivalent of 20 college football games (he missed more than half of his first game, against James Madison, following a head-over-heels crash landing, which caused him to miss the following game with UAB. He also missed half of the 2000 game against Pittsburgh, did not play that season against Central Florida, and played four brave series at Miami when he really shouldn't have been on the field). Imagine what he could have accomplished if he had stayed for his junior and senior seasons.

Nobody, however, could second-guess his decision to turn pro. The risk of injury was too great—injuries dogged him in both Tech seasons—and you can't do any better than No. 1.

Virginia Tech's potent combination of a great coach (Frank Beamer) and membership in a BCS Conference (The Big East) enabled it to compete in major bowls for the first time. But it was Vick who took the Hokies to the mountaintop. In 1999, he led Tech to the national championship game against Florida State, and the synergy surrounding that team spread. Season ticket applications grew, and Tech added a monstrous new south end zone, complete with luxury boxes, in 2002.

Michael Vick.

The Hokies knew they had a good player when they signed Vick. The *Roanoke Times* ranked him the No. 3 player in the state behind Ronald Curry (North Carolina) and David Terrell (Michigan). But they really didn't know what kind of player they had until he played in his first game. One of Vick's greatest attributes is his elusiveness, and in team drills, players were rarely allowed to hit him.

In retrospect, according to NFL draft status, Vick should not only have been the No. 1 player in the state; he should have been the top-ranked prospect in the nation—throughout a two-year span, if not more.

By the time he was a redshirt sophomore, Michael Vick was virtually a rock star. His dazzling performance on a national stage in the 1999 Sugar Bowl elevated him to superstar status, and fans hounded him almost everywhere he went.

There was a small retail shop in the lobby of the team's hotel in New Orleans. Vick popped in, and a group of fans followed him inside. That caused a mild stir, catching the attention of others. Before long the store was packed, and faces were pressed against the glass, trying to get a glimpse of him. The crowd grew to four or five people deep around the store and nobody could move. The manager finally had to call security to clear a path so Vick could leave.

The next season, Tech's first road game was at East Carolina. When the team arrived in Greenville, North Carolina on Friday, 50 people were in the hotel waiting for him. That's when Vick began using hotel service elevators to get to his room.

Michael Vick finished third in the Heisman Trophy voting after a spectacular freshman season and earned an invitation to the 2000 Espy Awards in Las Vegas. It was heady stuff for a 19-year-old.

His trip to Vegas began as a reality check. It ended in a surreal blur.

It was the middle of February. Sports information intern Bryan Johnston picked up Vick at his apartment around mid-morning, and they headed to Roanoke Regional Airport. Johnston had gotten to Christiansburg when Vick realized his didn't have a photo ID with him.

Delay No. 1.

When they arrived at the airport, they found that all the flights were canceled because of fog.

Delay No. 2.

Johnston left Vick at the gate to see what he could do. When he returned, Vick had the hood of his gray sweatshirt pulled up tightly around his head, surrounded by autograph seekers.

Johnston went to the desk. "Listen, we really need to get to Vegas."

"What's your name?" the airline official said.

"Well, my name is Bryan Johnston. But I'm traveling with Michael Vick."

"Oh." (Short pause.) "Let me see what I can do."

The official procured a van and driver who could take them to the Greensboro airport. Another desperate traveler rode along, spending most of the trip on her cell phone, saying, "You'll never guess who is sitting behind me!"

Vick just tried to sleep.

The van was winding down Rt. 220 when Johnston saw something come out of the woods, then heard a loud WHUMP. He turned to see a deer shaking its head and staggering back into the woods.

"What was that?" a groggy Vick said.

"Mike, we just hit a deer," Johnston said.

"Oh really?" he said, and went back to sleep.

They flew from Greensboro to Charlotte, where their flight to Vegas was postponed for five hours.

Delay No. 3.

It was all too much for Vick. He told Johnston he was ready to go home.

"Mike, we can't," he said. "Your mother [Brenda Boddie] has flown all the way from home [Newport News, Virginia]. She's waiting for you in Vegas. And, like, ESPN is sort of expecting you."

They finally arrived at the MGM Grand Hotel at 2 a.m—5 a.m. Eastern time. Vick was floored to find that even people in Las Vegas recognized him. With all the bright lights and excitement, Vick and Johnston suddenly weren't so weary anymore.

The next day Johnston learned that Vick won the ESPY as College Football Player of the Year. "Hey, Mike!" he said. "You won."

The first thing Vick said was, "Do I have to give a speech?"

As he dressed for the show that evening, Vick realized that his shirt sleeves were too short. Johnston, who was rushing to get ready himself, scrambled to find Vick a new tuxedo shirt. Then, when it was time to appear, ESPN had everything choreographed to the second; Vick took a hotel service elevator to the ground floor where a limousine took him around the block—just so he could walk down the red carpet.

"First time a limo ever took me to the hotel I just left," Johnston said.

When they emerged from the limousine, the first person they saw was Florida State head coach Bobby Bowden. "Man," he said to Vick, "I've seen enough of you already!"

Vick and Johnston were led to the green room, where Peyton Manning asked if he could sit with them. "I just have one piece of advice for you," Manning said. "When you go up on the stage to accept your trophy, don't trip."

Vick spotted Tiger Woods standing across the room. "I want to meet him," he told Johnston.

"Well, go on over and introduce yourself," Johnston said.

"Naw, man."

So Johnston went over and introduced himself to Woods, who said, "I'd love to meet Michael Vick."

After the two chatted, Vick shook his head. "I can't believe Tiger Woods knows who I am," he said.

Woods met Mark McGwire and Michael Jordan and Michael Johnson and a bevy of other sports stars. As they rode to the after-party in a limo with Kurt Warner and Sugar Ray lead singer Mark McGrath, Vick just kept shaking his head.

"I can't believe all these people know who I am."

After accepting his ESPY, Vick stood onstage with the likes of Woods, Warner, Andre Agassi, and Lance Armstrong. At the time it was heady stuff, but now it all fits. *Men's Journal* recently named Vick the world's No. 1 athlete—over the likes of Woods and Armstrong.

During Michael Vick's sophomore year, Bryan Johnston would receive 20 phone interview requests a week, and Vick really only had time to do five. When somebody would call on a Monday, requesting an interview for Wednesday, Johnston would have to cover the phone and hold it away so they wouldn't hear him burst into laughter.

"I've got an opening in three weeks," he told them. "Let's see. ... Tuesday at 2:15."

Inevitably, they took it.

Michael Vick and Tiger Woods pose for the camera at the 2000 Espy Awards in Las Vegas. *Photo courtesy of Bryan Johnston*

It got so bad, Vick started to hide when he heard Johnston was looking for him.

"It became a little game," Johnston said. "Every time I found him, he'd be smiling at me like a little kid."

Bryan Johnston had a routine for tracking down Michael Vick. First he would leave a note in his locker. Then he'd send him an e-mail. Then he'd call his apartment. An hour before the interview, he'd call Vick's cell phone.

Ah, the cell phone. When Michael Vick first arrived on campus, he'd give his number out to pretty much anybody who asked. But midway through his redshirt freshman season, the phone buzzed incessantly. "Oh my God, what have I done?" he thought.

"He changed his number three or four times after that," Johnston said.

Most Hokie fans might have this impression of Michael Vick as a very quiet, reserved person. "But around his friends, he's very outgoing," Bryan Johnston said. "A real clown. He's the kind of guy who will run around the locker room wearing nothing but a pair of sneakers, snapping people's butt with a towel."

And Vick can't function without his cherry Chapstick. He'd keep it in his thigh pads during games and couldn't do a TV interview without it. It started when he saw himself on TV and realized he was always licking his lips. To get them from getting dry, he began applying Chapstick, and it had to be cherry-flavored.

Before one of the 2000 Gator Bowl practices, there was a press conference to address the possibility that Vick would turn pro. In the locker room Johnston stood with Vick, who was holding a fresh container of Pringles potato chips. He asked to borrow Johnston's cherry Chapstick.

"Here, hold these for a minute," he said, handing the Pringles to Johnston. When he was done applying the Chapstick, he threw it into his locker.

"Hey, that's mine," Johnston said.

"You mind if I keep it?" he said.

"If you're keeping the Chapstick," Johnston said, "then I'm keeping the Pringles."

To Vick it was a fair trade.

During the 2000 season, sophomore quarterback Michael Vick had assured Tech's coaches he was staying for his junior year. But while the team was practicing for the Gator Bowl, Vick told a TV reporter that he was thinking about entering the NFL draft.

After practice, Frank Beamer asked John Ballein, "Have you heard that Mike might be reconsidering?" Ballein said no.

As part of the bowl festivities, the team was going to the dog races that night. Beamer had a prior engagement and met the team at the track. As he and Ballein approached the parking lot, there were about 30 TV cameras waiting for them.

"I guess there IS something to that story," Beamer said.

Vick really had no choice; he was going to be the first pick in the NFL draft. You can't do any better than that. To spurn that and return to Tech would have been madness. What if he had another serious injury? No matter what he accomplished, his status could only go down, not up.

"I remember leaving a press conference for the Gator Bowl at the Jamerson Center," Richmond *Times-Dispatch* writer Mike Harris said. "Vick was sitting in a lounge area outside the football offices with [defensive back] Ronyell Whitaker and about a half-dozen other players, bantering and laughing. They were having the best time. As I left, it dawned on me how much he enjoyed being in college. I think he really wished he could have stayed one more year."

Michael Vick's first year in Atlanta was mostly low key. He took over as starter in his second season, when he would have been a Virginia Tech senior. It didn't take long for him to start generating a buzz around the league. People all over the country were finding out what the Hokies had known for three years.

In a game against Green Bay, Vick was flushed out of the pocket. He scrambled to his right, just the direction you want a left-handed quarterback to go. When quarterbacks throw across the field, the ball loses momentum and defenders have more time to track it. The result is often disastrous. But with his body going one way, Vick flicked the ball across his body for a 28-yard gain. Diagonally, the ball probably went 40 yards on a frozen rope.

Atlanta defensive line coach Bill Johnson was watching this on film, and two plays went by before it sunk in. Wait a minute, he thought. I don't believe what I just saw. He rewound the tape.

"Will you look at this?" he told his players, taking a break from his lesson. "Just stop and look at this." The Falcons' linemen watched, slack-jawed. It was the only time all day when there was utter silence in the rowdy room.

"We were just in awe," said defensive end Patrick Kerney. "He's a freak. You know in X-Men, when the military realized Wolverine was invincible, with that Adamantium bonded to his skeleton? Well, we have to worry about the military kidnapping Michael to create a super-army of Michael Vick clones."

Quite a quote, considering Kerney went to UVA.

When people talk about Michael Vick, it's like film critic Roger Ebert analyzing his beloved *Citizen Kane*. "It's like God put all these great elements together and gave them to Mike," receiver Shawn Jefferson said. "He's got the arm of Dan Marino, the toughness of Bert Jones, the speed of Bo Jackson and the leadership ability of Terry Bradshaw."

Falcons personnel director Ron Hill said Vick is the best runner from scrimmage he has ever seen. "Once he gets in the open field, angles mean nothing," he said. "I was around Tony Dorsett [in Dallas]. He's bigger and stronger than Tony and accelerates better."

Edge NFL Matchup host Merrill Hoge makes a living watching NFL tape, and he says he never has seen anyone like Vick. "You always want to be careful to compare, but when I watch him run, the first person I think of is Gale Sayers," he says. "He's that fast, that fluid."

Said *Edge NFL Matchup*'s Ron Jaworski, "The first time I saw him warming up, I was blown away. He can make the zip throws, the touch throws, the soft toss over a linebacker, the long ball with the high arc that comes down through the chimney. He has the full complement. I've seen all of Donovan McNabb's games, and he still doesn't have all the throws. Week in and week out, Michael Vick can make more throws than Donovan McNabb."

Vick was drawing attention all over the country—all the way to Portland, Oregon. The Portland affiliate had been going back and forth between televising the Seattle Seahawks, San Francisco 49ers and the Detroit Lions (because of former Oregon Duck star quarterback Joey Harrington). But midway through the season it switched to Falcons games because Vick was such a drawing card.

Portland Oregonian media columnist John Hunt asked voice of the Hokies Bill Roth how Vick changed the way an announcer broadcasts a game.

"Well, when his team has the ball, you don't begin any stories," Roth said, "because when he's under center, he's in scoring position."

Hiring quarterbacks coach Kevin Rogers might prove to be one of the best staff moves Frank Beamer ever made. Without Rogers, Michael Vick's kid brother Marcus would not have come to Virginia Tech.

Rogers recruited Michael Vick for Syracuse and very nearly landed him. The Vick brothers took note of how Rogers handled Marvin Graves and Donovan McNabb and were impressed. When Rogers joined the Hokies' staff, Marcus figured he'd get the best of both worlds: a fabulous position coach and a school where his brother felt like part of a big family.

Michael never pressured Marcus to attend Tech, but it is evident he's happy with how things worked out. "There are only two differences between Marcus and me," he said on Halloween of 2002 [Vick or Treat!]. "I wore No. 7, and he wears No. 5. And I'm a lefty, and he's a righty. Those are the only differences you will see. I'm being honest!"

CHAPTER SEVEN

The Assistant Coaches

I t was 1978, Bill Dooley's first year at Virginia Tech. The Hokies were down by one or two points, with about a minute left in the game. It was fourth and one, and Billy Hite, Tech's new running backs coach, was at the edge of the coach's box on the sideline, trying to get a better view. He heard Dooley yell, "Billy! Hey BILLY!"

Hite was excited. Here was Coach Dooley, asking HIM what to do in this critical situation. Hite ran over and Dooley drawled, 'Hey, Billy, you got an extra cigarette?'"

Tech's defensive ends coach in 1987 was former Hokie player Duke Strager, he of the signature line, "It is only an insult if you perceive it to be true." Known for his outgoing personality, Strager was a guest on WSLQ radio that fall. Head coach Frank Beamer gave him just one bit of advice: "Don't embarrass the program."

For the most part Strager succeeded, but he did manage to zing his boss. "I want to wish a happy birthday to Coach Beamer," Strager announced. "He's going to be 62 years old this Sunday."

When Strager returned to his office later that morning, he found a note taped to his door.

It read: "The 62-year-old man wants to see you in his office at once."

The Hokies were coming off a bitterly disappointing 2-8-1 season in 1992, and head coach Frank Beamer was forced to make several coaching changes. One of them was promoting graduate assistant Bryan Stinespring to a full-time coaching position.

Everybody knew, however, that if Beamer couldn't turn things around, he would probably be gone, too. Tech opened its season with a 33-16 win over Bowling Green, then traveled to Pittsburgh to take on the Panthers. The game was considered a tossup.

The night before the game, Stinespring, sharing a hotel room with assistant Billy Hite, was understandably nervous.

Stinespring got in bed and Hite shut off the light.

"Coach Hite, are we going to be all right tomorrow?" he said. "Are we going to be all right?"

The room was deathly quiet.

"Coach Stinespring," Hite said, "This will be the biggest game of your entire life. If we don't win, we'll probably all get fired. Now get a good night's sleep."

Ten seasons later, Bryan Stinespring was Virginia Tech's offensive coordinator. His first season (2002) began a little shakily, however; the Hokies didn't want to put first-year starter Bryan Randall in too many difficult situations, so the offense was conservative, upsetting many fans.

During the season the Stinesprings were enjoying a family meal. "Honey, I know you don't like to do this," said Bryan's wife, Shelly, "but could you please PASS the potatoes?"

Before a game at Boston College, Bryan Stinespring was a nervous wreck. Offensive coordinator Rickey Bustle could see him sweating. "Two things, Stinespring," he said. "No. 1, your seat is against the wall, and that's good, because when you pass out, it will stop you. No. 2, it's a good thing John Ballein has put your name on your press pass, so the EMT people will know who you are when they take you out of here."

Before every game, John Ballein would put a quotation in everybody's locker. It was a Tuesday and he was looking for a good quote to use for the weekend.

"Why don't you use carpe diem, said assistant coach Bryan Stinespring.

"Carpe diem," Ballein said. "What in the hell does that mean?"

"What, you never saw the film *Dead Poets Society*?" Stinespring said.

"I'm not that much into movies."

"I cannot believe a man of your intelligence does not know what carpe diem means. Seize the day!"

"Bryan," Ballein said, "I guarantee you that the next guy who walks through this door won't know what it means."

"You have a bet," Stinespring said.

Just about then assistant coach Tommy Groom walked in.

"Tommy," Ballein said, "do you know what carpe diem means?"

Groom laughed. "Oh yeah," he said. "That's the money they give you when you drive your dealer car. You know, car per diem."

Rickey Bustle came to Tech with Beamer in 1987 and was Tech's offensive coordinator in 1993. He went to South Carolina for one year before returning in 1995. He became head coach at Louisiana-Lafayette in 2002.

An intense competitor whether he's playing racquetball, golf, or coaching football, Bustle, too, had a tendency to sweat before games. It was even worse when the Hokies played at Clemson, because

Bustle played for the Tigers. Before the game he was dripping buckets up in the coach's booth, and he took off his shirt and began scratching himself.

"Oh Lord," John Ballein thought, "please don't let the camera pan up here right now."

When Rickey Bustle woke up at 5:30 the morning of Tech's 1995 game at Rutgers, it wasn't to get a head start.

"I didn't know if I was dying," he said, "but it sure felt like it."

He was suffering from a kidney stone. Team physician Duane Lagan checked him out and had him rushed to the St. Peter's Hospital emergency room in New Brunswick.

They hooked him up to an IV and gave him some demerol, but the thing that was killing him the most was not knowing the score of the game. Eventually his wife called the hospital and told him the Hokies were ahead 7-3.

The stone eventually moved to a less painful position, and when the Demerol wore off, he was released. He got to the stadium at halftime.

"The first thing he said to anybody," said John Ballein, "was, 'Did my bags get on the bus?'"

With Rickey Bustle out, assistant coaches Billy Hite and Terry Strock were charged with calling Tech's plays. "I was walking down the hotel hallway this morning, and someone said,'"Hi Diddle Diddle, run it up the middle,'" Hite said, referring to the old Bill Dooley adage. "Then I got a lecture from Coach Beamer this morning: No Dooley Ball."

One year a Hokie player had been consistently missing his 8 a.m. entomology class, which Rickey Bustle simply could not understand.

"Why is he taking an insect class that early?" Bustle said. "He needs to take it when the bugs are flying around."

In 1999, Bustle gave Beamer his evaluation of one of Tech's backup quarterbacks.

Said Bustle, "He's the third best of the two."

A year later, the Hokies faced the Hurricanes in Miami with an injured Michael Vick.

"How's the game plan going?" Beamer asked Bustle before the 41-21 loss.

Said Bustle, "I feel like I'm having to cut down a redwood tree with a hatchet."

Every football season, the Blacksburg Sports Club invites a coach to speak at its Wednesday luncheons. Prior to the 1993 Boston College game, it was tight ends coach Bryan Stinespring's turn. He planned to bring his wife, Shelly, who worked in the football office. A little bit before noon he walked down the hall.

"Ready to go?" he said.

"Bryan, for the last three Wednesdays I've been eating at Macado's with [administrator] Sharon McCloskey and [assistant coach] Billy Hite. Would you mind if I went with them instead?"

Stinespring knew the Hokies were in the middle of a three-game winning streak.

"No honey, not at all," he said. "In fact, here's $20. Order dessert!"

Graduate assistant James "Bubba" Brown was the Blacksburg Sports Club's featured speaker the week of Tech's 1994 game with North Carolina State.

"I'm sure you all have heard the graduate assistant horror stories," he said. "Washing coaches' cars, picking up their laundry, making food runs to McDonald's. I'm here to say it is nothing like that. I have not once ever picked up any food at McDonald's."

In 1991, the Hokies were coming off a difficult home loss to East Carolina. Starting quarterback Will Furrer's knee locked up on him during pregame warmups, so backup Rodd Wooten was pressed into action. On the first drive of the second half, Tech, leading 14-7, had driven to the ECU four-yard line. Coach Frank Beamer sent in a "locked" play, which means the quarterback is not supposed to audible out of it. But Wooten saw something in the Pirates' alignment that made him think the play wouldn't work and called a pass.

Pirate free safety Greg Grandison intercepted it and ran 95 yards for a touchdown, tying the game. Tech never recovered and lost 24-17, dropping its record to 5-5 with the season finale at Virginia remaining.

Furrer was out for the Virginia game, so the staff had to make a decision on whom to play: Wooten or redshirt freshman Maurice DeShazo.

Beamer left it up to his offensive coaches and wanted a decision by Thursday.

When Thursday rolled around, he asked offensive coordinator Steve Marshall who was going to play quarterback.

"I think we should go with DeShazo," he said.

Beamer asked quarterbacks coach Rickey Bustle. "I'm not about to change quarterbacks again now," he said. "We should stay with Wooten."

He asked Tommy Groom and Bryan Stinespring, and they split the vote. Graduate assistant James Brown would have to break the tie.

"Bubba," Beamer said, "what do you think?"

"Coach," he drawled, "You ain't paying me enough to make this decision."

In 1994, assistant coach Terry Strock was fussing at holder Jon Shields for talking during a practice drill.

"I'll give you my shirt and whistle if you want to do the coaching," an angry Strock said.

Without missing a beat, Shields said, "What about your house?"

Beamer knew the 1999 game at West Virginia was going to be a tough one. Morgantown is always a tough place to play, and he was worried that his undefeated, third-ranked team might take the 10-point underdog Mountaineers (3-4) lightly. So instead of the regular Friday night video, Beamer asked some players and coaches to speak. He chose tailback Shyrone Stith and defensive tackle Nathaniel Williams, because they were generally quiet; their words word carry more impact. He chose assistant Jim Cavanaugh, because in all of his years of coaching he had pretty much seen everything. He chose graduate assistant Chris Malone, a former player. And he chose secondary coach Lorenzo "Whammy" Ward, a former Alabama defensive back who played in the 1989 national championship game against Miami (the 1990 Sugar Bowl).

Everybody stood and spoke for about 30 seconds about how the game was going to be a "war" and a "slobber-nocker."

Then Ward stood up.

"Gentlemen!" he said. "You heard what these men have said. This game is going to be a WAR! Tomorrow, we are going to have to play the game of our lives!" And he stood there, looking at everybody.

Good speech, Beamer thought, and started to get up from his chair. Then Ward spun around on his heel.

"And GENTLEMEN!" he continued, "I want to tell you this! Those fans will be on you like no fans have ever been on you!" And he stopped and stared around the room.

Beamer started to rise from his chair again.

"And GENTLEMEN!" Ward continued, and his allotted 30 seconds turned into three minutes, with a couple more "gentlemen" thrown in, and the legend of the Rev. Whammy Ward was born.

The Hokies had a couple of close calls in their perfect 11-0 regular season of 1999. One came at Pittsburgh, where Panther quarterback David Priestley torched the Tech secondary for 407 yards in the Hokies' 30-17 win.

It had been a tough day for defensive backs coach Lorenzo "Whammy" Ward. When he boarded the plane to go home, he asked the flight attendant how far it was from there to Blacksburg.

"About 500 miles," she said.

"Damn, Whammy," said graduate assistant Billy Houseright. "that's about what Pittsburgh threw on us tonight."

As they waited for the plane to take off, Ward's cell phone rang.

"It's probably [Pittsburgh coach] Walt Harris," an assistant said. "He wants to buy you a beer."

After the season, the coaches were talking about whom they should vote for on the All-Big East squad. "I thought that quarterback from Pittsburgh was pretty good," Ward said.

Said Beamer, "I guess you do."

One spring, some prominent alumni invited the coaches to play golf on the Eastern Shore. Charley Wiles was in a foursome with Whammy Ward, John Ballein, and J.C. Price and had a dogleg-left par 5, over water. You could lay up, or you could try to cut the corner by going over the water, which was a pretty good distance away. "I'm going to play this one safe," Wiles said, and pulled out his seven-iron.

He hit the ball poorly. "Aw," he said, "I should have tried to carry it over the water."

"Just see if you can do it," Ward said.

Wiles pulled out his driver and mashed it, the ball settling in the middle of the fairway.

"There you go, Charley, there you go," Ward said. "Hindsight is 50-50!"

Charley Wiles, Tech's defensive line coach since 1996, was a former All-America player for Frank Beamer at Murray State. He has a unique way of expressing himself, and through the years longtime buddy John Ballein has scribbled down some of Wiles' best lines.

Once Wiles asked one of his players: "Did he visually see you?"

One day Wiles was updating Frank Beamer on a top recruiting prospect. "Coach Beamer, this kid has narrowed his choices down to four."

"Great, Charley. Who are they?"

"Clemson, UNC, Tennessee, Virginia and Virginia Tech."

Another time, Beamer had asked him about another player Wiles was recruiting. "I talked to the kid last night," Wiles said. "He told me he would LOVE to be interested in Virginia Tech."

Later on Beamer asked Wiles what he thought the chances were of landing the prospect.

"I'm optimized," he said.

As a Hokies assistant, Wiles made his first flight to Boston College in 1996. As the plane approached Logan Airport, Wiles looked through the window and saw a strip of land about 100 feet wide. "Hey, look, Bud," he said to coach Bud Foster, "I think that's Long Island."

Frank Beamer, who was sitting in front of Wiles, grunted. "Charley," he said over his shoulder, "we're going to Boston, not New York."

"Aw," Wiles said, "I don't know much about geology."

CHAPTER EIGHT

The Rivalries

In the modern era, all Virginia Tech has ever wanted was a single home for its athletics teams. But the lack of foresight by the school's early leaders and administrators was responsible for the Hokies' seemingly always-tenuous conference status.

In 1932, a mood of de-emphasizing athletics prevailed in Blacksburg. After 10 consecutive winning seasons, VPI slipped to a 3-4-2 mark in 1931. Coach Orville "Slippery" Neal, suffering from constant pain in his foot from an old war wound, missed several games, then married a coed and left campus. That, for sure, will leave a sour taste in a president's mouth.

"The real aim of our football and all our athletics is the development of physical fitness and moral character in our students," president Dr. Julian Burruss said. "If we fall short of this greater aim, we fail. If we achieve it, we win, and the score of the game makes only minor difference."

You can imagine the response from today's Hokies: "Like HELL!"

The 1932 team featured a halfback, Al Casey, who could do 50 one-armed pushups, and a one-eyed receiver, Al Seaman. Only about 18 players saw action. But the team finished 8-1 in the Southern Conference, creating a buzz across the region.

To appreciate this, you have to remember what the Southern Conference was like in 1932. The original 1920 roll call went like this: Alabama, Auburn, Clemson, Georgia, Georgia Tech, Kentucky, Maryland, Mississippi State, North Carolina, North Carolina State, Tennessee, Virginia, Virginia Tech, and Washington and Lee. Tech was part of the clique.

In 1922, Florida, LSU, Mississippi, South Carolina, Tulane, Vanderbilt, and VMI joined. (Imagine the Hokies as a league member before Florida and LSU!) Sewanee joined a year later, and Duke joined in 1928.

These were the biggest names in southern football, and VPI's football squad was among the elite.

But in the early 1930s, there was a rift. Roughly half of the schools wanted to take football to the next level; they wanted radio broadcasts and they wanted to raise money for athletics scholarships. The other half, led by VPI's own Sally Miles, insisted on keeping a ban on athletics fund-raising. Miles also named Henry (Puss) Redd, Tech's freshman coach who served as the school's alumni secretary, as the new head football coach. Redd had the same idealogy as Miles. "To me, nothing is more discouraging than to see a young man perform brilliantly on the athletic field," he told a cheering student assembly after he was hired, "and then, at the end of his college year fail to earn a diploma with his class."

In December 1932, the 13 members west and south of the Appalachian mountains reorganized as the SEC: Alabama, Auburn, Florida, Georgia, Georgia Tech, Kentucky, Louisiana State, Mississippi, Mississippi State, Sewanee, Tennessee, Tulane, and Vanderbilt.

With a different mind-set, VPI might have been part of that group.

That left the 10 "coastal" schools to conduct themselves in their hoity-toity manner: Clemson, Duke, Maryland, North Carolina, North Carolina State, South Carolina, Virginia, Virginia Tech, VMI, and Washington and Lee. At least it was perfect geographically.

In 1949, Tech president Walter Newman was also president of the Southern Conference, and he frowned upon such frivolous postseason pursuits as bowl games. Balderdash, he thought! That's unnecessary time away from the classroom! His Hokies, with their proper academic mind-set, finished 1-7-2 that year.

The year before, Clemson went undefeated and beat Missouri in the Gator Bowl. In 1950 the Tigers went 9-0-1 and beat Miami in the Orange Bowl. This did not sit well with Miles, so before the 1951 season, the Southern Conference passed a rule banning bowl particpation. The ban incensed Clemson coach and athletic director Frank Howard; the Tigers, along with Maryland, ignored the rule. Things got testy.

In the spring of 1953, Clemson, Duke, Maryland, North Carolina, N.C. State, South Carolina, and Wake Forest withdrew to form the ACC. That December, the league admitted UVA. Tech was left out, in part because it had one of the worst football programs in the country during the 1940s.

But it was also left out because Frank Howard wasn't happy with Newman. After that bowl fiasco, he was determined to block Tech's invitation to the ACC.

One of the great stories in Hokies lore came in 1986, when the 0-1 Hokies traveled to Clemson's Death Valley, where they had not won since 1954. Tech was a two-touchdown underdog and had lost nine in a row to the Tigers.

It was a hot, sun-washed September Saturday, and the ACC network televised the game.

"All you could see was orange," said defensive end Morgan Roane, "and all you could hear was noise."

As per tradition, before the game Clemson players stood at the top of the hill in one end zone, where they each rubbed "Howard's Rock"—named for that same Frank Howard who blocked Tech's bid—before descending to the field.

"Look at that," linebacker Paul Nelson said. "Let's wave their [butts] down here. Bring 'em on!"

Fellow linebacker Lawrence White, standing next to Nelson, figured that would look good for TV. So he joined Nelson. In seconds, the rest of the team followed their lead.

"We wanted to show those [77,000] Tiger fans we weren't scared," Roane said.

Longtime Clemson sports information director Bob Bradley said he had never seen a team do that before. The stunt irked head coach Bill Dooley, who growled, "If you do something like that, you better be able to back it up."

Placekicker Chris Kinzer booted field goals of 31 and 38 yards, defensive back Mitch Dove recovered a blocked punt in the end zone for a score, and quarterback Erik Chapman threw a five-yard scoring pass to tight end Steve Johnson. The defense did the rest as Tech pulled the upset, 20-14.

Two years later, Frank Beamer brought his team back to Death Valley, this time before a crowd of 80,500. Many of the players on his squad had heard the now-legendary story of the wave, so they thought it would be a great idea to try it, too.

"Great," Beamer said. "Let's get them even more riled up."

Then Beamer took a closer look at the players doing the taunting. They were all second-stringers.

Clemson won 40-7.

In 1989, Beamer experienced chest pains during a game at East Carolina. That week he checked into Roanoke Memorial Hospital for a transluminal coronary angioplasty, which relieved a nearly 95-percent artery blockage. After the procedure there was a press conference at the hospital, and a reporter asked if stress contributed to his heart problem.

"I'll tell you what stress is," Beamer said. "Stress is being on the operating table and realizing that three of the four doctors around you are West Virginia graduates."

The first time Frank Beamer's Hokies played Florida State was 1988, when the Seminoles were ranked No. 5 and featured defensive back Deion Sanders. It was the players' first trip to Tallahassee, and they kept hearing the stories about FSU mascot Chief Osceola and how he would ride onto the field on his big Appaloosa horse and thrust a flaming spear into the turf at midfield.

The story was too much for excitable linebacker Don Stokes. Before the game he had worked himself up into a frenzy, cursing and punching lockers and telling everybody within earshot that when that (bleeping) horse came onto the field, he was going to (bleeping) tackle it.

Beamer wasn't sure how to handle this situation. Yeah, he wanted his players fired up to play FSU. But, geez, tackling a freaking horse? He thought it over and pulled aside assistant coach Billy Hite.

"I want you to take care of Don for me," he said.

Hite nodded, started to walk away, then turned back toward Beamer.

"Coach," he said, "what, exactly, do you want me to do?"

Beamer wasn't sure himself.

When they got on the field, and the Appaloosa came charging out, Beamer kept a close eye on Stokes.

"Billy," he said into his headset mic, "Don's getting closer to that horse."

Beamer kept watching.

"Billy, he's edging closer."

Hite clicked on his headset mic. "Coach," he said, "if Don Stokes is determined to tackle that damn horse, there's not a whole helluva lot I'm gonna be able to do about it."

Hite dutifully followed Stokes, who never did tackle the Appaloosa.

"Maybe he got up close to it," Beamer said, "and realized how big that thing really was."

Frank Beamer could be forgiven if he had nightmares about that horse. He dropped four consecutive games to Florida State from 1988-91, then lost to the Seminoles in the 1999 national championship.

The most galling loss came in 1991, the final regular-season game of the series. It was scheduled for Blacksburg, but the Seminoles offered athletic director Dave Braine an $800,000 guarantee to move the game to the Citrus Bowl in Orlando. A home game would have netted about $350,000, and Tech's athletics department was financially strapped at the time. Braine elected to take the $450,000 profit.

The Hokies outgained the Seminoles 420-343 but lost a fumble and three interceptions and lost 33-20. But the worst part came before kickoff, during the FSU introductions.

The stands were filled with garnet and gold-clad fans doing the tomahawk chop as players such as Marvin Jones and Terrell Buckley came strutting out, leading a pack of hugely muscled athletes. "Geez, look at the size of these guys," Beamer muttered. Then he saw the worst thing of all.

The damned Appaloosa horse.

Beamer lost it. "Dammit, they're not supposed to have that horse here!" he screamed to the officials. "This is OUR home game!"

In the press box before Tech's 1993 14-13 loss at West Virginia in Morgantown, a local reporter looked over the Hokies' roster. "This guy should be playing for the Mountaineers," he said. "Bryan Still."

In the 1974 Tech-Virginia game at Scott Stadium, the Hokies were down 28-14 in the fourth quarter. Quarterback Bruce Arians' one-yard run made it 28-21 with 7:44 left, and then with no time left, his 11-yard touchdown pass to Ricky Scales made it 28-27. The Wahoos protested, unsuccessfully, that Scales' foot was out of bounds.

Tech, naturally, went for the win. Arians called an option to the right, following a block from halfback George Heath.

"I landed waist-high in the end zone," Arians told the *Hokie Huddler.* "All of our guys are yelling that we had won the game. By now I'm at the bottom of a big pile, then I hear UVA start to scream that they had won the game. I'm still lying under there with the ball in the end zone, but the officials ruled no score.

"The linesman was supposed to make the call, but he was nowhere to be seen. The other referees didn't say anything; they just ran off the field."

The most frustrating thing, Arians said, was that he never got an explanation. According to *Hoos 'N' Hokies: 100 Years of Virginia/Virginia Tech Football*, Arians knew one of the officials from high school, Brian McDevitt, who became a lawyer in Philadelphia. "We knew you scored," he told Arians, "but Scales was out of the end zone."

Hokies offensive lineman Stuart Plank remembers two teams being exceptionally tough and physical: West Virginia and Memphis State.

"Those were tough dudes," he said. "They didn't care if they lost, as long as they hit you."

Their fans had the same mentality. Plank remembers sitting on the bench at Memphis when a liquor bottle whizzed by his head. He nodded to a teammate and without saying a word put on his helmet.

It happened again, this time in Morgantown against the Mountaineers. "The only difference was, this time the liquor bottle was empty," he said. "I respected that."

Stuart Plank said the West Virginia fans were brutal. "It was like going to the Vet to play against the Eagles," he said. Virginia, on the other hand, "was like going to a Lakers game."

"It's one thing for a big dude in overalls cursing you from the stands. But you almost have to laugh when a guy is giving it to you and he's wearing short pants, a tie and a blue and orange beanie cap."

Virginia Tech was a 10-point underdog to Virginia in the 1985 game at Scott Stadium, and indeed found itself down 10-0 at halftime.

"We need to quit trying to throw the ball," the all-senior offensive line of Stuart Plank, Kent Thomas, Mark Johnson, Tom Mehr, and Scott Cruise told coach Pat Watson. "Please tell Coach Dooley we can run all day on these guys."

He did, and Dooley listened. Thirty-nine of Tech's 46 second-half plays were runs, including 22 in a row in one stretch. Tech outgained Virginia 241-57 after halftime and went on to win 28-10.

"The guys on the other side of the ball were starting to lose it, yelling at each other," Plank said. "We even started telling them what play was coming, and that just made it worse."

Virginia Tech was having its way with Syracuse during the 1986 game in the Carrier Dome. Its offense had been moving up and down the field so much that by the second quarter the players were exhausted. "It was so loud in there, and we could barely breathe," fullback Sean Donnelly said.

They were lined up in the I-formation, and Donnelly was watching the football through the legs of quarterback Erik Chapman and center Bob Frulla. Tailback Maurice Williams lined up behind Donnelly. Over the din, Chapman screamed, "Ready! Set!"

Defensive end Bruce Smith.

Just then Frulla threw up on the football before snapping it.

"In a nanosecond, I heard Maurice groan behind me," Donnelly said. "Then the Syracuse guys starting laughing. Maurice went up the middle for about three yards, and everybody was laughing but Maurice. He was wiping his hands on his jersey and going, 'Oh, man, that ain't funny.'"

The Hokies made the decision to switch from white shoes to black for the 1991 season, but the 1990 seniors wanted to wear the white shoes for their last game. They had bought several cans of black spray paint and, just hours before the big game against Virginia, were outside the Jamerson Center, spraying their shoes black.

Equipment manager Lester Karlin had a fit and went to Frank Beamer, who remained calm. "Just make sure everybody is wearing the same color," he said.

Virginia had been ranked No. 1 that year. Tech went into the game 5-5 against a tough schedule. When Beamer went back to his office, he thought, "Geez, we're about to play Virginia, and our players are worried about the color of our shoes. They're either going to play awful, or they're going to play great."

Tech, wearing all-maroon uniforms for the first time since 1984, won 38-13.

"We figured the shoes would throw Virginia off," said linebacker Archie Hopkins. "And it gave us a meaner image."

Meaner—or uglier? "Maroon shirts, maroon pants and shoes spray-painted black," Beamer said, shaking his head. "That was about the ugliest-looking team I've ever seen."

That 1990 game in Lane Stadium was played before a record football crowd (54,157) for the Commonwealth of Virginia. Spirit was high, with plenty of banners. But one stood out.

The Cavaliers had a wide receiver named Derek Dooley. This banner read: "No Dooley has ever made a passing game work in Lane Stadium, and they're not going to start today."

Dooley dropped two passes in the game.

While the all-maroon worked in 1990, the reverse was true in 1994 when the Hokies opted for all-orange. They had eight turnovers as the Wahoos won 42-23. Quarterback Maurice DeShazo had five interceptions, and teammates gave him some serious ribbing about it afterward. "The next week, at dinner, somebody asked me to pass the salt," he said, "then they said, 'Nah, forget it. It would probably get picked off before it gets here.'"

At Virginia in 1995, longtime Cavalier trainer Joe Gieck stuck out his leg as cornerback Antonio Banks returned an interception for a touchdown to seal Virginia Tech's dramatic 36-29 comeback win.

UVA athletic director Terry Holland called Tech AD Dave Braine the following day and apologized for the faux pas. Aw, there was no need. All Tech fans knew Gieck was just doing the Hokie-Pokey: "I put my right foot in, I put my right foot out.... That's what it was all about."

Former Hokie pitcher Brad Clontz was barely a month removed from celebrating the 1995 World Series title as a member of the Atlanta Braves when Tech beat Virginia the same year. Standing outside Tech's locker room at Scott Stadium after the game, he was asked what was sweeter: the World Series ring or Tech beating Virginia?

He had to think about it.

Before the Sugar Bowl, a writer from Texas, Mark Wangrin, was looking for teams who had played both Texas and Virginia Tech and get their thoughts on who was better: Longhorns end Tony Brackens or Hokies end Cornell Brown. Virginia played both, and he quoted senior Cavalier quarterback Mike Groh.

"There's no comparison," Groh said. "We didn't change anything in our blocking scheme to try to stop Cornell Brown. We did for Tony Brackens."

The quote wasn't the first time Groh had gotten himself in the Hokie doghouse. Earlier that season a local TV station taped Groh, who remarked that Tech was lucky to have beaten the Cavaliers that season.

"I was surprised to hear him say that, him being a coach's son," said Tech center Billy Conaty. "I wonder if he would have said those things if he was a junior."

Now that Mike's father, Al, is head coach at Virginia, things probably make a little more sense to Conaty.

Groh wasn't the only one disparaging the Hokies that season. ESPN's Lee Corso had implied that New Orleans had better brace itself for a mass invasion of country bumpkins, assuming Tech fans can get their John Deere tractors jump-started, and turn Bourbon Street into Bubba Street. He picked Texas to win, but after the game, Frank Beamer got the last word as the Hokies won 28-10 to finish 10-2.

"As long as Mike Groh and Lee Corso keep picking against us," he said, "we'll be all right."

Cornell Brown and Tiki Barber fight for the ball outside of Hotel Roanoke.

One inventive fan's sign features characters from the well-known TV show *South Park*.

During one stretch of the undefeated 1999 regular season, Virginia Tech knocked out the opposing quarterback in five consecutive games. The defense, led by defensive end Corey Moore, knocked Miami quarterback Kenny Kelly from the game on three separate occasions. "I was hurting pretty bad," Kelly said.

In 1999, Virginia was ranked No. 24 and had beaten the Hokies two years in a row. With the game at Scott Stadium, the Cavaliers were confident of extending the streak to three.

It was not to happen. Less than six minutes into the game, wide receiver Andre Davis beat Tim Spruill deep and quarterback Michael

Vick hit him in stride for a 60-yard bomb. By halftime, the No. 8 Hokies led 28-7 and it could have been worse; they fumbled just before halftime. The final was 31-7, but some Wahoos were still in denial.

"They're overrated," said offensive tackle Brad Barnes. Cav co-captain Noel LaMontagne said Brigham Young had a better defense, and that Tech was "a big fish in a little pond."

A good ole boy in Roanoke heard that comment while relaxing in his favorite bar. "If Tech is a big fish in a little pond," he drawled, "then UVA just took a three-hour tour on the USS *Minnow*."

Tech defensive end Corey Moore had a retort with less convoluted logic. "Look at the scoreboard," he said. "That's a woodshed."

As in where you go to get a spanking.

The quote became a mantra for Tech's undefeated season, inspiring the author's brother to song:

Ode to the Woodshed/Steve Colston

Oh Woodshed, the bane of each Tech foe.
Oh Woodshed, where each opponent must surely go.
Oh Woodshed, you welcomed J-M-U
Oh Woodshed, the Blazers went there too.

Oh Woodshed, Clemson felt the pain.
Oh Woodshed, you made U-V-A complain.

And Rutgers took their whipping
Within your Woodshed walls
Syracuse could not refuse
When it heard your Woodshed call.
The Panthers fought, but it was all for naught
The Woodshed they could not survive.
Through seven games, the Woodshed reigned,
The score was two-ninety to sixty-five.
Only in West Virginyer, where the sheep do quiver
Was there no need for that shed of wood.

To the Mountaineer faction, the Woodshed looks like a mansion,
If they move in, there goes the neighborhood.
Oh Woodshed, a Hurricane cannot blow you down.
Oh Woodshed, Temple kneeled upon your hallowed ground.
Oh Woodshed, you made the Eagles wish they'd never hatched.
Oh Woodshed, for you the Seminoles have no match.

Oh Woodshed, to you I raise my glass
Oh Woodshed, here's to whuppin' ———!

CHAPTER NINE

The Media

In 1986, Virginia Tech had just beaten Clemson at Death Valley for the first time since 1954. It seemed like a big upset at the time, considering the Hokies had lost their opener at home to Cincinnati.

It was Thursday, September 18, and Tech fans were still reveling in the win when the *Roanoke Times* broke stunning news: head coach Bill Dooley had filed a $3.5-million lawsuit against the university for breach of contract. That evening after practice, he told his team this would be his last season in Blacksburg.

Earlier that year, Dooley claimed, university president William Lavery had told him his dual positions of athletic director and head coach would be terminated. After further negotiations, the university determined it was willing to keep him on as coach but not AD, which Dooley found unacceptable.

Roanoke Times & World-News writer Jack Bogaczyk had gotten the tip earlier that day. He grabbed reporter Blair Kerkhoff and they raced to Montgomery County Courthouse. Newspaper reporters regularly check court records, but Dooley had worked a deal with the judge to seal his document and it never made the "out" basket. Since it was a matter of public record, the reporters prevailed.

Bogaczyk looked at his watch. "If we hurry," he said, "we can get to Dooley before practice starts."

With Kerkhoff speed-reading the lawsuit copy—which was about 20 pages long—Bogaczyk flew toward Blacksburg at 80 mph. Their tires squealed as they turned up Spring Road, just as Dooley and assistant coach Sandy Kinney were crossing the street.

"I'll never forget the look on his face when we drove up," Kerkhoff said. "It was like, 'Oh, shit, what do THEY want?'"

The car had not yet rolled to a stop when Kerkhoff jumped out, scrambled to his feet and sprinted toward Dooley, who said, "I can't comment on this."

"We wrote a 100-inch story," Kerkhoff said, "and Dooley didn't say a damn thing."

It was all so bizarre: Dooley had filed a $3.5-million suit against his employer, yet was still coaching the team. Fire him now? He just beat Clemson!

"The crazy thing," Bogaczyk said, "was that not one of his assistants knew about the lawsuit. When I broke the news to assistant Jim Tait, I thought his legs were going to buckle."

Don Lloyd Fleeger—air name Don Lloyd—was the first broadcaster to call both Tech football and basketball games on a consistent basis. He was the voice of the Hokies from 1974-82. Ken Haines, the school's director of public affairs, served as Lloyd's color analyst.

The two were in the middle of a broadcast when Dr. Wilson Bell, a Tech Hall of Famer and the faculty chairman of athletics, visited the booth and saw a phone off the hook. Bell figured he'd be helpful so he hung up the phone—knocking Lloyd and Haines off the air.

During one Tech-Virginia broadcast, Don Lloyd turned to Ken Haines and said, "You know, Ken, when these two schools meet, you can throw the record books out the window."

Haines said that was true indeed, grabbed his media guide—and tossed it from the booth.

Under Ken Haines, Tech's radio network tripled to more than 50 stations statewide in the 1970s. And it wasn't a collection of schmoe, low-watt stations either. He had WAVA in Arlington, Virginia, WSLC in Roanoke, WRVA in Richmond and WTAR in Norfolk. "I told them Virginia Tech was a school that was ready to take off," he said. "I said it was going to be a dominant power, sooner rather than later. We also promised that our coaches would do promos for the stations."

One year there was a young woman interviewing for a position on the sports information staff. She had fine credentials and had done well in her initial interview with director Jack Williams.

"I think she is a strong candidate," Williams told his staff. "I'd like to have another interview session, where you all will be free to ask her some questions."

The young lady showed up for her interview in Williams' office; the five members of the sports information spread out around her.

"What duties do you expect to perform in this position?" a staff member asked her.

"Well, I was talking to Mr. ... um...HIM," and she extended her arm, pointing her index finger at Williams. "And HE said..."

She did not get the job.

Jack Williams served as Tech's sports information director from 1978-98. He also served as sports information director at North Carolina, as well as assistant sports editor of both the *Atlanta Journal*

& Constitution and *The News & Observer* of Raleigh. After leaving Blacksburg he joined the Georgia Tech Sports Information Office as sports information director emeritus.

Williams always emphasized loyalty and he was passionate in his love for Virginia Tech. He was also intense; when he focused on a task, nothing could deter him.

In 1985, Tech played Florida in Gainesville. The Gators won 35-18, and the team just wanted to board the plane and get home as quickly as possible. It was Williams' job to usher the Hokie broadcast team of Jeff Charles and Mike Burnop from the press box to the bus in timely fashion. On this afternoon the postgame show went slightly long, and Williams became nervous. He knew Dooley could be impatient and might order the buses to leave without them.

Charles and Burnop packed up and hurried down to the field, which they had to cross; the buses were waiting beyond an end zone ramp. "Hurry! Hurry!" Williams said, focused on the task at hand. "We've got to GO! We've got to GO!" At about the 50-yard line, the clasp on Charles' briefcase sprung open, and the phone they used for the broadcasts bounced onto the grass and its bell rang. Burnop picked it up and put the receiver to his ear. "Jack, it's for you!" he said, handing the receiver to Williams.

"Hello? Hello?" Williams said. "Burnop, there's nobody there... ah, you [jerk]!"

Longtime Tech sports information director Dave Smith celebrated his 40th birthday September 7, 1988, and when he arrived at his office that morning he found it decorated with black balloons and banners that read, "Over the Hill."

Several of his co-workers, including Tech administrator Vito Ragazzo, gathered at his desk to sing "Happy Birthday" and enjoy some cake. That's when some fresh doughnuts arrived at assistant Sharon Spradlin's desk in the adjoining room.

"Hey, Vito!" Spradlin said, aware of Ragazzo's sweet tooth, "We have doughnuts out here!"

"Oh, great," Smith said. "Do they have 'Over the Hill' written on them, too?"

"No," said Ragazzo, "but they're stale."

In 1992, *Richmond Times-Dispatch* writer Mike Harris had what he described as "the summer from hell." He had lost 35 pounds in one month, and doctors couldn't figure out what was wrong with him. "It's like I've got an incurable virus," he told sports information director Jack Williams during Big East Media Day at Giants Stadium. Williams, who was standing with Tech running back Vaughn Hebron, suddenly remembered he needed to give some information to commissioner Mike Tranghese and told the players, "Don't move. I'll be right back."

Harris coughed again. "Incurable virus, huh?" said Hebron, who began edging away.

ESPN's College Gameday loves coming to Blacksburg. In 1999 Chris Fowler, Lee Corso, and Kirk Herbstreit made their first visit to Lane Stadium and drew a then-record turnout for their pregame show. They were so impressed they returned a few weeks later for the Hokies' game with Miami.

They were also on hand for the 2000 season opener with Georgia Tech that was canceled because of lightning. Corso had predicted a Hokies loss, and just before kickoff, a lightning bolt struck his rental car.

"I don't know what a Hokie is," Corso said, "but God is one of them."

ESPN's *College Gameday* with Chris Fowler, Lee Corso, and Kirk Herbstreit.

Bill Roth hosts the *Hokie Hotline* each week during football season with coach Frank Beamer. One evening Roth introduced him by saying, "this is such a wonderful show, Coach. Every Monday night, you get to expose yourself to thousands of Hokie fans!"

"Well," Coach Beamer said, "I don't know about that, Bill."

Mike Burnop used to do his postgame interviews with Coach Beamer on the field immediately after the game. This practice ended after the 1989 season.

In the opener, Tech beat Akron 29-3 in a game where a player ran into Zips coach Gerry Faust on the sideline. He finished the game on crutches, and afterward, when he went to meet Beamer at midfield, Burnop's mic picked up Faust exclaiming, "[Bleeping bleep], Frank, your guys broke my [bleeping] leg!"

Later that season, at Virginia, a fight broke out after the Cavaliers' 32-25 win, and Beamer, trying to break it up, caught an errant elbow flush in the mouth from one of his own players, defensive end Jimmy Whitten. Beamer thought, "This is a helluva thing. Our biggest rival just kicked our butts, people are swarming

The crew of *ESPN's College Gameday* has some pregame Hokie fun.

all around me and I'm on my hands and knees, looking for my right front tooth."

With mayhem all around him, Burnop wondered, "Why am I on this field? I'm in the middle of a melee at Scott Stadium with a Tech shirt on. I need hazard pay for this!"

Roth, still up in the press box, was unaware of what happened. "And now let's go to Mike Burnop, who is on the field with Coach Beamer," he said.

"Well Bill," Burnop said, taking a deep breath, "right now Coach Beamer is on his hands and knees, looking for his tooth."

Beamer valiantly forged through the interview, although he couldn't say his "Fs."

After what he had been through, that was probably a good thing.

Bill Roth and Mike Burnop refer to each other as the "Buffet Buddies," and Burnop's eating exploits are particularly legendary. "He thinks the Gaza Strip is a steak," Roth said.

In a 1994 trip to Hattiesburg to play Southern Mississippi, the two had dinner at a place called "Catfish Hatties" that featured a seafood buffet.

"PTP," Burnop said.

"Huh?" said Roth.

"Prepare to pound," Burnop said.

Roth and Burnop each mowed through about 8-10 plates, loading up on the spiced shrimp.

Then it was time for dessert, and the restaurant had a soft-serve ice cream machine. "Why mess with a bowl?" Burnop joked. "Let's just put our mouths under the tap."

Etiquette prevailed, and as they took their mounds of ice cream back to their table, a smattering of awed Hokie fans gave the two a standing ovation.

One year, when the Hokies were playing at Miami, Bill Roth and Mike Burnop went to a Heat game to see former Tech star Bimbo Coles. It was a close game and the crowd began chanting, "Let's go HEAT! Let's go HEAT!"

"These are my kind of people," Burnop said.

"How so?" said Roth.

"Listen to them," Burnop said. "They're yelling, 'Let's go EAT!'"

Tech had a brutal road schedule in 1991. In one five-game stretch, the Hokies traveled to North Carolina State, South Carolina, Oklahoma, West Virginia, and Orlando to play Florida State. The wacky schedule took its toll on everybody.

After the Sooners game a 27-17 loss Bill Roth and Mike Burnop stayed late to take calls for *The Point After*. Usually, they followed the Hokie team buses with their police escort to the airport. But this time the show ran long.

Roth did his best to make up for lost time, driving on the shoulder and zipping in and out of traffic. They ran through the airport terminal lugging their heavy radio gear, only to arrive at the gate to see the plane rolling down the tarmac—along with their personal luggage.

Naturally, the first thing Roth and Burnop did was to find someplace to eat.

It was on that road trip that Burnop and Roth had gone to Cattleman's Steak House in Norman. They sat down in a nice booth. On the wall over Burnop's shoulder was an oil painting of a large steer.

The waiter arrived and asked, "What will you have?"

Burnop pointed to the picture on the wall. "I'll have him, medium."

That same season, the Hokies played Navy in Annapolis. Bill Roth and Mike Burnop checked into the Marriott and immediately hit the lunch buffet. The lunch rush was over and the room was largely empty. At the end of the buffet was a serving pan full of sliced flank steak. Nobody was manning the buffet, so Burnop took a set of tongs from the table and scooped up half of the steak in the pan. Roth did the same thing.

When the buffet chef returned from the kitchen, he looked at the empty pan, and looked around the room, empty except for Burnop and Roth.

"You should have seen his face," Burnop said. "He looked around and saw only two people and couldn't figure out what happened to all that meat."

The buffet Mike Burnop will never forget came during the 1996 Orange Bowl. Officials rented the Miami SeaQuarium for the official parties of Tech and Nebraska. Burnop and Bill Roth found a spread that featured filet mignon, pork ribs, lobster and stone crab claws.

"You've got to be [bleeping] me," Burnop said to Roth. "They're going to turn us loose in here?"

Although this was ostensibly a social event, the two didn't talk to anybody else for the next two hours. "We camped," Burnop said. "We were in our own little world and didn't say a word to anybody. How could we? Our mouths were full."

In a 1995 game at Navy, the Midshipmen band played "Anchors Aweigh." During a commercial break Mike Burnop started humming along with the song, and when it was over, Bill Roth left Burnop's microphone on. "The only words I knew were 'Anchors Aweigh,' and I can't really sing," Burnop said. The Hokies won the game, and on *The Point After,* fans called in and told Burnop to keep his day job.

The following week Tech played the Akron Zips, so Burnop sang "Zippity-Do-Dah," and the Hokies won again.

Soon the media began picking up on the gig. The *Richmond Times-Dispatch* ran a feature on Burnop's choice of melodies each week.

As long as Tech won, Burnop would sing. And as long as he sang, Tech kept winning. It put together a 10-game winning streak, and Burnop kept churning out the hits, changing the lyrics to suit the opponent.

Tech 27, West Virginia 0: "Take Me Home, Country Roads"

Tech 31, Syracuse 7: "New York, New York."

Before the Hokies played Texas in the Sugar Bowl, coach Frank Beamer promised he would sing along with Burnop if his team won. So after the 28-10 victory over the Longhorns, Beamer and Burnop performed a duet to the tune of the "The Yellow Rose of Texas":

Oh the Hokies went to New Orleans
To play a football game

The Sugar Bowl had chosen
The teams to entertain.
The Texas guys were awesome,
Self-assured and unafraid.
The Hokies were just happy
To be in the parade.
But the Yellow Rose of Texas
Has turned Maroon tonight
The Hokies beat the Longhorns
This game was outta sight!

Mike Burnop is one of those people everybody loves. In 1992, on the Friday before Tech's game at Louisville, Burnop and Bill Roth arrived at the office of Cardinals head coach Howard Schnellenberger for an interview.

There was a snafu, because when the administrative assistant notified Schnellenberger that the radio people had arrived, he snorted, "I don't know anything about this."

"They're on the schedule, Coach," she said.

"Well, OK, send them in," he said, "but make it quick. I'm very busy."

Schnellenberger pulled out his pipe and asked them to sit down. Burnop asked him about his pipe tobacco, and one thing led to another. He and the coach hit it off. An hour later, they were still in his office, with Roth looking at his wristwatch and thinking, "We've got to get out of here or we're going to miss dinner."

The Friday before the Hokies played at Florida State in 1988, Bill Roth, wearing his nice black dress shoes, stepped into a puddle. He wasn't quite sure, exactly, what kind of muck he had stepped in, but the next morning, the sole had separated from the shoe.

"Hey Mike, look at this," he told Burnop. "I've got a flapper."

Roth figured he could fix it with a little duct tape, which he always keeps with his radio gear. But after three steps, his shoe was flapping again.

"I can fix that," Burnop said.

He wrapped the gray duct tape all around the heel of Roth's black dress shoe.

"Just don't tell anybody about this," Roth begged.

"Sure," Burnop shrugged.

They arrived at the stadium and set up without incident. About an hour before game time, Tech athletics director Dave Braine, now the AD at Georgia Tech, visited the booth.

"Hey Dave!" Burnop said, before Braine had a chance to say hello. "Check out Bill's shoe!"

For the 1994 Gator Bowl, then-WSLS-TV (Roanoke) sports staffers Greg Roberts and assistants Darren Triplett and Tyler Potter left the station on Christmas at 11 p.m. and drove through the night to Jacksonville. They arrived in time to film the football team coming off their plane.

In all, Potter had been on the road for 16 consecutive hours, since he had spent the holiday with his parents in Connecticut. "It was a blur," Potter said. "I kept wondering what state I was in."

Said Lynchburg sportswriter Gary Crockett, "Probably in a state of delirium."

Roanoke Times sportswriter Randy King was driving home from the Big East Media Day on I-81 when a blue Chrysler Intrepid with Pennsylvania tags suddenly swerved into his lane. King bounced off the guard rail and came to rest in perpendicular fashion. The Intrepid kept motoring. An 18-wheeler smoked his tires to a halt, jumped from the cab and began waving down a pack of oncoming vehicles.

According to his account in his online *Roanoke Times* column, VT Insider, King was unhurt, except in his wallet: A few months earlier, he persuaded his wife to drop the full-coverage insurance on the 1997 Saturn he was driving.

He was driving his wife's car instead of his own beloved 1991 Chevy Lumina because the Saturn got better gas mileage. At 27 cents per mile, he would make about $225 after deducting his $35 gas outlay.

Now, instead of making two-something, he was losing two-something—with a comma included.

To make matters worse, the Rockbridge County folks sent him a bill for $973 to repair the guard rail.

Coming out of high school in 1980, *USA Today* sportswriter Skip Wood knew he wanted to be a newspaperman. A freshman, he had been on campus two days when he attended a *Collegiate Times* organizational meeting at Squires Student Center. All the different editors made their spiels, but the one Wood will always remember is CT sports editor Steve Woodward. He got up in front of the crowd with five or six cigarettes jammed in his mouth, to show how stressful journalism could be. Then he asked if anybody in the crowd wanted to work for the sports department. Wood and few others raised their hands.

"That's fine. We'll be happy to give you a tryout," Woodward said, "on one condition."

It was a condition that would immediately knock out anybody who bought this book.

"If you are a Tech fan," Woodward said, "you will not work for my sports department. We are not a homer paper. We not only want to compete with the *Roanoke Times*, we want to try to kick their ass.

"If you want to write for me, your allegiance to the Hokies ends now."

Wood took those words to heart. He started off as a reporter and became sports editor. After some freelance work that included covering Tech football for the (Christiansburg) *News-Messenger*, he took a job with the *Harrisonburg Daily News-Record*, where he covered Tech football from 1986-88. From there he took a job with the *Richmond Times-Dispatch*, where he covered the Hokies from 1993-96. He covered Tech's appearance in the 1999 Sugar Bowl for *USA Today*.

Throughout his successful rise in journalism, Wood had maintained his objectivity. But with his alma mater about to face No. 1 Florida State in the title game, it finally hit him. He was returning to his seat with a plate of food in his hand when he heard that old familiar song. The Marching Virginians were blaring, "Tech Triumph," and Wood froze in his tracks.

"Determined now to win or die;

So give a Hokie, Hokie, Hokie Hi!

Rae Ri, Old V-P-I!"

The Tech fans roared, and a chill went down Wood's spine. "Freaking Virginia Tech is about to play for the national championship," he said to himself, thinking back over the last 20 years, all the ups and downs, with more downs than ups. And he shook his head.

"I'll be damned."

CHAPTER TEN

The Fans

Although *Animal House* is the greatest movie about college ever made, we all know it would have been even better with a tailgating scene in it. Still, it did feature a road trip, and road trips are a big part of what makes college football the greatest sport of them all.

According to Jerr Rosenbaum of the laugh-out-loud hilarious web site Tailgatefever.com, nothing says "Go Hokies!" like a bowl game road trip. And sometimes it is the small bowls that deliver the biggest memories.

"Take the 1998 Music City Bowl, Nashville, Tennessee," Rosenbaum said. "Whoever decided to put a bowl game in central Tennessee in the middle of winter—great idea! Great as in 'Great, it's 14 degrees' or great as in 'Has anyone seen my great big ski parka?'"

Rosenbaum and four of his closest football buddies made the 10-hour trek, passing the time by challenging each other to name every mascot in Division I-A.

Through careful and judicious planning, Rosenbaum's crew managed to procure five of the very worst seats Vanderbilt Stadium had to offer, which allowed them to fully appreciate the wind, rain, sleet, and even a little snow. "We are talking the drop a penny off the back of the stadium, not a single inch of cement to block the wind—

Hokies fans are among some of the most loyal in college football.

the very top of the stadium," he said. To get an idea of this brutal weather, think Apocalypse, minus the locusts.

"By halftime there was no denying it: only a complete fool — or an undergrad—would stay out in this ice storm," Rosenbaum said. "There comes a point in every man's life when he loses that internal struggle between desire and reason. Sadly, this was our day." With the score 10-7, the crew left in search of cold beers, which actually warmed them up, and they learned one of the best things about SEC football: they put bars right next to the stadium. "Outstanding," said Rosenbaum, who observed, "Rector Fieldhouse would make an excellent bar."

The beer search proved to be the game's turning point. Corey Moore had a terrific second half, setting up two scores with a quarterback pressure and a blocked punt. The Hokies routed Alabama 38-7, their first-ever victory over the Crimson Tide. Finally, revenge for sending them Jimmy Sharpe!

Rosenbaum and company defrosted in Cooker's Bar & Grill, where they watched this fabulous second half. A Tennessee fan taught them the words to "Rocky Top," which they then insisted on singing every time Tech scored (blame that on the beers). "We learned two valuable lessons that day," he said. "No. 1, never leave a game early, something exciting might happen; and, No. 2, do not sing 'Rocky Top' to Alabama fans. They will find this neither amusing nor entertaining."

Jerr Rosenbaum's
10 Greatest Things About Virginia Tech Football

1. The Cannon. Where else do they fire a warning shot to let you know you have time for one more drink before leaving the tailgate?
2. Have you seen our cheerleaders?
3. 8 p.m. kickoffs.
4. At most schools, punts are considered a chance to beat the bathroom rush; at Tech they are legitimate scoring opportunities.
5. Burnt orange. Who doesn't look good dressed head to toe in burnt orange?
6. The 1993 Independence Bowl. The Sugar Bowl is great but this one started it all.
7. Bill Roth (you've got to love this guy... even though he came from Syracuse).
8. The third quarter of the 2000 Sugar Bowl.
9. People doing the hokey-pokey, outdoors. Priceless.
10. That Tech has a space reserved in the Merriman Center for the national championship trophy.

Tailgatefever.com started as an e-mail between friends. In 1995, Jerr Rosenbaum was a law student at the University of Richmond. He got caught up in the excitement of Tech's Sugar Bowl season and felt compelled to regularly update a fraternity brother in Florida on the Hokies' latest accomplishments. The e-mail list quickly expanded to about 10, and word of mouth took over. Soon Rosenbaum started getting requests from fans wanting to be added to the list.

Rosenbaum's brother, Dan, created a web site in 1998, and now the site gets between 2,000 and 3,000 hits per week during the season.

Before games, Rosenbaum said, people will often come up to him and say, "You've got to check out this web site, Tailgatefever.com. It's hilarious!" Sometimes he'll just smile and say, "Oh yeah? I'll have to do that."

Although Lane Stadium is football nirvana for Hokie fans, away games present an often-overlooked opportunity for tailgating. Even though you're not in one of the wonderful lots around Lane Stadium, a road game is still a football game, and wherever there is a football game, there should be tailgating—even if you are just watching the game at home. "That eliminates all sorts of tailgating burdens," said Tailgatefever.com's Jerr Rosenbaum. "Things like driving, packing, hotel reservations, and bathing."

Road games are great, he said, because "nobody knows you, which presents limitless possibilities. And a huge road game, such as at Texas A&M, can be like a bowl game in the middle of the season."

In 2002, Rosenbaum, Tray Allen, Tim Allen (not the actor) and Mike O'Connell made that trip to College Station, Texas. "Until you've convinced your Continental Airlines flight attendant to allow you to lead the plane in LET'S GO! HOKIES! you haven't really lived," Rosenbaum said.

But they almost missed the flight, because on the way to Ronald Reagan Washington National Airport, O'Connell insisted that they stop so he could buy a brand-new Lee Suggs jersey.

"A new jersey!" Rosenbaum said, and he wasn't talking about Rutgers. "What are you talking about? You already have a Lee Suggs jersey."

"Not a white jersey."

"A what?"

"This is a road game. We wear white on the road. I'll look ridiculous wearing a home jersey on the road."

A Suggs jersey, a VT hat, a pair of VT socks and a sweet pair of sunglasses later, they were back on their way.

Upon landing at George Herbert Walker Bush Intercontinental Airport, they were directed to Gate B86C for their connection to Easterwood Field. They had to take a train to get there. "This airport was eerily reminiscent of the Jetsons cartoon we watched earlier that day," said Rosenbaum, who observed that most gate listings incorporating a letter corresponding to the terminal and a gate number in that terminal. "It was the 'C' in 'B86C' that concerned us," he said.

They took numerous turns, circles, and ramps, passed several confused mice, and arrived at a large waiting room for Gates B86A, B86B, and B86C. Outside there were buses.

"Are you bussing us to College Station?" Rosenbaum asked.

"No sir. The buses are so you don't get run over by other planes on the tarmac."

In the end, they didn't take a bus to the plane, because the bus was actually larger than their plane: An Alenia ATR42.

"On board are 20 Tech fans, 11 Texas A&M fans, one pilot, one steward, and 14 chickens," Rosenbaum said. "God bless Texas!"

O'Connell turned to Rosenbaum, with a crazed look in his eye. "What the hell have you gotten us into?" he said.

But the ride was smooth; the ATR42 flew like a bird. "A dying bird with one broken wing crying out for help," Rosenbaum said. "Top speed, 60 MPH."

Twenty-three terrifying minutes later, they arrived.

Aggie football is steeped in tradition. One of the traditions is the "yell practice" held at midnight before games; 40,000 people attend this event. "So during the game," Rosenbaum said, "all of their cheers are well-organized. Freakishly so. Come to think of it, A&M fans kind of resemble a cult on Saturdays. They gather in large areas, wear prescribed uniforms, and chant nonsensical phrases. Basically, everything that is done more than once at A&M becomes a tradition, and these traditions are taken very seriously."

O'Connell informed several fans that it was once a tradition in America not to drive cars, then added, "But we didn't take a horse and buggy to the game."

The Aggies responded with blank stares.

Tech's locker room entrance was right by the visitors' seats, so the foursome hung out hoping to meet some players. It was there that they literally ran into Tech defensive coordinator Bud Foster. O'Connell grabbed him by the shoulders and yelled, "Give 'em hell, Bud!" To their surprise, instead of summoning security, Foster gave O'Connell a high-five.

At the end of the game, fans crowded the path to the locker room to celebrate the victory. Player after player high-fived the fans. When Lee Suggs came by he noticed O'Connell's jersey, pointed to it, then to his, and gave O'Connell the biggest grin you've ever seen, as if to say, "Hey, nice road jersey."

Eighteen months later, O'Connell was still riding the natural high. "Sometimes, he actually believes he is Lee Suggs," Rosenbaum said. "He took it very personally when Suggs was not drafted in the first round. When he wears the jersey he makes us call him Lee. He says, 'I'm not Mike; I'm Lee. Call me by my name!' Ridiculous, yes, but that's the college game."

Exuberant Virginia Tech students stormed the Scott Stadium field in 1983 after Virginia Tech's 48-0 hammering of Virginia and tore down the goalposts. They took a section of the crossbar and got the idea that it would be really great to show it to the Hokie players in their locker room. They arrived to find the door locked. Undeterred, they used the bar as a battering ram, trying to bust down the door.

The fans celebrate alongside the players in the 1995 Sugar Bowl.

That's when head coach Bill Dooley stuck his head out, as if he were answering the door for a sales call. "It's OK to celebrate," he said, "but you can't be bringing that thing in here."

The 1993 Independence Bowl was Tech's first postseason football victory since 1986 and left many fans giddy with joy. One student, who had been over-served in his celebratory carousing, crossed paths with star Hokies wideout Antonio Freeman, who had five catches for 66 yards, including a 42-yard touchdown.

"Hey man, can I call you 7-Eleven, man? Can I? Huh? I wanna call you 7-Eleven."

"Sure, man," Freeman laughed. "Whatever."

The student stood there, waiting. Freeman started to walk away.

"Hey, wait, man," the student said.

"Yes?" Freeman said, turning.

"Don't you wanna know why I wanna call you 7-Eleven?"

"OK. Why?"

"Because," the student said, grinning, "you're open 24 hours a day!"

In 1994, hundreds of Hokie students lined Washington Street outside Cassell Coliseum, camping out for tickets to the Virginia game. During the middle of the week, coach Frank Beamer and assistant John Ballein brought them 20 gallons of coffee and 40 dozen doughnuts. As Ballein went through the row of tents, rousting the students, a weary camper stuck his head out into the cold and said, "Do we have to wait in line for the coffee, too?"

On November 4, 1995, Syracuse visited Blacksburg for one of the most-hyped Hokie home games ever to that point. ABC televised the game, its first trip to Lane Stadium since 1981. The Orangemen, led by sensational freshman quarterback Donovan McNabb and star wide receiver Marvin Harrison, were ranked No. 20 nationally, but the Hokies rolled 31-7. Quarterback Jim Druckenmiller had a big day, throwing for 224 yards, three touchdowns and no interceptions. Fans rushed the field and tore down the goalposts.

Autograph seekers besieged Druckenmiller. A fan standing next to him asked to hold his helmet for him as he signed, and in the melee Druck sort of nodded. When he had finished signing, however, the helmet was gone.

During the ensuing TV interviews, Druckenmiller pleaded for the fan to return his helmet. The next morning, Druck received a phone call.

"If I bring back your helmet," the contrite voice said, "you're not going to kick my butt, are you?"

Quarterback Jim Druckenmiller.

A little bit later, Druck heard voices outside his door. Then there was a knock. "I think they were trying to decide whether to leave the thing at the door, ring the bell and run," he said.

Buoyed by some cohorts, the fan opted to stay, apologizing ad nauseum. Then he asked if Druck would mind signing his ticket stub.

Druckenmiller even obliged him when he asked if he could pose for a few photographs with him and his buddies.

Roanoke Hokie fan Mike Shaver couldn't get tickets to the 1995 game at Virginia, but that didn't stop him from heading to Charlottesville with his good friend Ken Brickey. They milled around the crowd outside the gate but refused to pay the scalpers' fee of $75.

Game time approached and they started to panic. Suddenly they heard a familiar sound: The Virginia Tech fight song. There, emerging from the parking lot, came the Marching Virginians. Shaver looked in the opposite direction and saw a security guard wrestling with the lock on a chain-link fence. "It was if it was happening in slow motion," he said. "I turned to Brickey and yelled, 'We're going in with the BAND!'"

Shaver jumped into the tuba section, but Brickey hesitated and the moment was lost. One of the tuba players looked at Shaver and said, "Who are you?"

"I'm a Tech fan from Miami who drove all night to get here," he said.

"Cool," said the tuba player.

In minutes Shaver found himself on the field at Scott Stadium and found a nice spot on the grassy knoll.

"It was like being in war with the bullets flying, and you had to make the decision to run or fight," Shaver said. "It was a defining moment in my life."

Mike Shaver and Sigma Nu fraternity brother John Keller traveled to Clemson for Tech's 1984 game against the Tigers that featured the nation's top two Outland Trophy candidates: Bruce Smith and William "The Refrigerator" Perry. The night before the game they went to a local watering hole and told anyone they saw, "If the Fridge walks into this bar right now, we'll kick his butt."

Said Shaver, "The Clemson fans didn't have a sense of humor about that."

After the game Shaver and Keller were hungry and began roaming about Memorial Stadium. "I want to get into one of those skyboxes," Keller said.

"We can't go up there," Shaver said.

"If you act like you belong," Keller said, "then you do belong."

They came to a turnstile with a guard. Keller looked him in the eye authoritatively and the guard let them pass to the suite level. After opening a few doors, they found that the South Carolina legislature box was empty. It was decorated with orange shag

Hokie fans celebrate on Bourbon Street.

carpeting and orange sofas and a TV. There were still food and mixers spread out on the counter.

They helped themselves to a snack and relaxed on the sofa, watching a baseball game on TV. A member of the cleaning crew stuck his head into the room, and Keller chastised him. "What are you doing?" he said. "Can't you see we're still in here?"

The cleaning person apologized and closed the door.

An estimated 32,000 Tech fans traveled to New Orleans for the 1995 Sugar Bowl. On the bus ride from the Le Meridien hotel to the Superdome, the driver clicked on his microphone. "I can't believe how many of y'all came down here to our beautiful city," he said. "There must not be anybody back in Virginia. You know what? When I drop y'all off, I'm gonna get on a plane and fly to Virginia and rob all of your houses."

A fan near the back yelled out, "I have a black Labrador retriever guarding my house."

"That's OK," the driver fired back, "I'll steal him, too."

On New Year's Eve, 1996, fans sat on the bus, waiting to go to the Orange Bowl game at Pro Player Stadium to see No. 6 Nebraska vs. No. 9 Virginia Tech.

"I hate to hurry up and wait," said an older Hokie fan from Pulaski. "It makes me so irritated, I think I will have to drink a beer."

His buddy next to him said, "Hell, if you get downright aggravated, you might have to drink yourself two or three."

CHAPTER ELEVEN

View from the
Huddler Desk

ow, I'd like to share with you a few stories from my 11 years behind the desk at the *Hokie Huddler* from 1985-96. In June of 1985 I replaced Doug Waters, who left after the paper's first year to become city editor at the *Winchester Star*. The *Huddler* lost $40,000 in its startup season, even though the football team went 8-4 and earned an Independence Bowl bid. Box office star Bruce Smith graduated, and the Hokies faced a reloading year. In my favor was a luxury Waters did not enjoy: the benefit of an assistant. I hired Mike Ashley, who, ironically, helped start my career, in a way. When Ashley left the *New Castle Record* to take an SID post at Radford University, publisher Ray Robinson hired me to take Ashley's place. We both grew up in the Roanoke Valley, and working a floor above Bill Dooley was heady stuff—as in over our heads.

In the fall of 1985, the *Roanoke Times & World-News* was running an extensive five-part examination of the Virginia Tech athletic department's financial problems. I had been on the job for four months when I opened the Monday, September 30, 1985 paper and turned to page B4. There was my picture in the paper, eyes wide, looking like a deer in headlights. Beneath the photo was the caption: "Editor Chris Colston knows subscriptions have to pick up to secure the future of the *Hokie Huddler*." Wait, it gets better. Over my mug was the headline, "*Hokie Huddler*: 'Positive idea' still far from break-even point." Senior writer Jack Bogaczyk's lead graf said, "The *Hokie Huddler* has billed itself as a newspaper devoted to coverage of Virginia Tech sports. For all intents and purposes, however, the Virginia Tech Athletic Association has had to bill itself for the *Hokie Huddler*."

Gulp!

A little further down in the story, Bogaczyk wrote, "the future of the *Huddler* is questionable" and posed the question, "How long can the *Huddler* continue losing money and be kept afloat by an athletics program that has other financial problems?"

Good question, I thought. I would kind of like to know that myself.

Call it naïve youth, but with less than two years of journalism experience at quite possibly the smallest weekly newspaper in the state, I nevertheless felt fully qualified to quickly bring the *Huddler* into the black. Apparently so did athletic director/head coach Bill Dooley, because in the story he said, "the projections are that [the *Huddler*] will pay for itself this year."

Dooley wasn't just blowing smoke. On more than one occasion that fall, business manager Don Perry told me, "If you guys don't turn a profit this year, you're likely going to be out of a job."

Other than that, there was no pressure whatsoever.

"We'd sit in that office, reading about how we would be out of a job in a year, and wondering if the power would be turned off at any minute," Ashley said. "Which would have been bad, considering the dreary room we called an office had no windows. It might have been years before anybody discovered us."

My primary duty was filling the paper with interesting content, a full-time job in itself. But I was also responsible for increasing circulation, selling ads, lining up photographers, delivering the papers to the mailroom—everything short of actually slapping on the mailing labels.

On the back page of the paper, we created the *Hokie Huddler* Restaurant Guide. The idea was to get area eateries a cheap way to get their name in front of fans coming into town for the game. We drew up a little map and sold the boxes for $25 apiece.

"Talk about a wake-up call," Ashley said. "I found out I couldn't even sell a $25 ad to a restaurant that would be going out of business in three months.

"This one place, Cricketts, used to drive me crazy. The manager tried to write a novel every week. Hey, pal, you're paying a measly $25! Let it go!"

Our job became a little harder when the football team started the '85 season 0-3. We never knew how long the restaurants would keep advertising with us, so we'd try to eat at as many of them as we could. Some of the places were struggling. There was this rib joint called Dem Bones; we'd be the only ones eating there.

"I remember working on that first regular-season issue on a Saturday night, listening to the game on the radio," Ashley said. "The Hokies lost to Cincinnati, and I thought to myself, 'Damn, there goes Dem Bones.'"

This was a typical work week from that first football season, and I swear, I embellish not a word:

MONDAY

Deliver *Huddlers* to mail room, distribute copies around the Jamerson Center and selected dorms. Eat lunch at soon-to-be-defunct restaurant advertiser. Take phone calls from irate fans wanting Bill Dooley fired. Take more phone calls from fans wanting to know the latest recruiting scoop. Read in *Roanoke Times* how the athletics department is in the red and will dump the *Hokie Huddler* next fall. Drink heavily.

TUESDAY

Make futile effort to sell ads. Try to figure out a way to increase circulation, realize I have no clue, and throw hands up in exasperation. Go to football press conference at Sheraton Red Lion

Inn. Eat free food. Count number of times Bill Dooley says "football" and "from the standpoint" and "style-play." Take phone calls from irate fans wanting Dooley fired. Take more phone calls from fans wanting to know latest recruiting scoop. Take even more phone calls from irate fans whose *Huddler* is late. Try to transcribe notes from the press conference before phone rings again. Realize it is impossible. Go home and do shots.

WEDNESDAY

Just like Tuesday, only busier.

THURSDAY

Repeat to self: This is my dream job. This is my dream job. Drive to Galax to work on the paper. Ask self, why is the *Huddler* printed in Galax? Try not to forget floppy disks that contain all copy. Get home by midnight. Open refrigerator, pray there is a cold beer waiting.

FRIDAY

Slam java. Travel with team to road site. Eat free box lunch and think, "This is a great job after all." Find a good sports bar and ask the waitress if they sell pitchers of Kamikazes. Loudly sing "Signs" by the Five Man Electrical Band and "Whole Lotta Love" by Led Zeppelin with other writers. Avoid bars with mirrors, as it is easy to think the person across the room is staring at you, but when you go over to ask the dude what the hell is his problem, it turns out he's you.

SATURDAY

Wake up, gleeful that nobody in Blacksburg witnessed previous night's behavior. Momentary euphoria quickly erased by raging headache. Slam java. Pray game is not in Morgantown, which means gruel for lunch in the press box. Try to stay awake as Hokies run sweep-style play for thirty-third time. Go to locker room. Find Carter Wiley and listen to him rant for 10 minutes. After subtracting all curse words, have five minutes' worth of usable quotes. Board bus. Eat greasy, albeit free, fried chicken. Wipe fingers on play-by-play sheet. Go to bed knowing next day will be total hell.

SUNDAY

Drive to Radford and pick up Mike Ashley. Drive to Galax. Ask self, why is the *Huddler* printed in Galax? Lose 2,000-word story by accidentally hitting wrong key on keyboard. Realize floppy disk with the other 2,000-word story is sitting on counter in Blacksburg office. Lay out paper. At 3 a.m., see 10th typo of the night. Contemplate suicide. Fix typo, drive to Radford, and watched Tech football show at Ashley's house. Go home and collapse in a heap, knowing the next day the fun starts all over again.

We were in our mid-twenties, working 65-hour weeks with no days off. We had little money, so we had to find creative ways to blow off steam. During those long nights producing the paper at the *Galax Gazette*—we learned it was a deal Bill Dooley had worked out in 1984—we invented a football game of our own. One of us would stand on the far side of the newsroom with a roll of toilet paper; the other would sit on a computer chair with rolling wheels. When the quarterback said "hike," the guy in the chair would push off and the quarterback would try to lead him. The receiver had to catch the roll before bumping into a counter.

Mike was very good at it. He could throw the softest roll of toilet paper you'll ever catch.

In our Blacksburg office, I bought one of those plastic kiddie basketball hoops at Kmart. This was the Larry Bird model. Mike and I would compete in fierce one-on-one games, banging into desks and knocking over books. Voice of the Hokies Jeff Charles had an office next door; he heard the commotion and popped his head in our office to see what the hell was going on. Being a natural basketball fan, he began to watch, then started doing play-by-play.

"Hearing Jeff Charles say 'Ashley for two … it's good!' was one of the greatest thrills of my life," Ashley said.

The *Huddler* lost $31,065 in 1985. Mike Ashley had signed a nine-month contract, which, because of our financial straits, was not renewed. I was on my own, and the pressure was still on. In the *Roanoke Times* follow-up story a year later, I said, "I've been told that we have to come close to breaking even or we won't return."

At least Mike didn't have to worry about Dem Bones anymore. He landed on his feet, getting a job in the sport information department that actually paid more than the pittance the *Huddler* could afford.

In December of 1986 he accompanied the basketball team to Richmond for the holiday *Times-Dispatch* basketball tournament. The members of the traveling party all received a nice tan parka with a sewn-on tournament logo. "I wasn't making any money," Ashley said, "so I could really have used one of those." But when he talked to a Tech official, he was told there weren't enough parkas for everybody.

A month later, as he was leaving Cassell Coliseum, one of Bill Dooley's sons walked past him—wearing one of those nice tan parkas. "After that," Ashley said, "I knew where I stood on the old totem pole."

I always tried to attend the Blacksburg Sports Club luncheon on Wednesdays. The treasurer was Ralph Cecchini, whose son John was a fraternity brother of mine. Ralph and I always enjoyed joking with each other. The price of the luncheon was $5, and one day I didn't have any cash so I wrote him a check. As I signed it, I told Ralph, "You better hold on to this check. It might be worth something one day."

"Well," he said, "it had better be worth $5 right now."

At the 1986 Peach Bowl, the Virginia Tech traveling party stayed at the downtown Hyatt Regency Hotel, while North Carolina State stayed at the adjacent Marriott Marquis. Don't get me wrong, the Hyatt was beautiful. Still, all week, we all had just a little bit of Marquis envy.

The next year, in May of 1985, the Chicago Cubs had a series scheduled at Atlanta. Former Hokies baseball star Johnny Oates was the Cubs' bullpen coach, thus presenting a fine opportunity for one of the *Hokie Huddler's* "Where Are They Now" features. I booked the trip, reserving a room at the—yes!—Marriott Marquis. The trip was a success, particularly the Marquis' breakfast buffet featuring melt-in-your-mouth croissants, plump apple Danish, fresh-squeezed orange juice and made-to-order omelets.

A few months later, the Buffalo Bills were scheduled to play an exhibition game in Atlanta against the Falcons. Again, a "Where Are They Now" opportunity presented itself in the form of star defensive end Bruce Smith. When I booked my Marquis room this time, there was good news and bad news. The good news was that I got a room for Friday and free breakfast buffet coupons for Saturday and Sunday. The bad news was the hotel was booked Saturday.

Oh, no problem, I thought; Atlanta has countless hotel rooms. I'll find something.

CT sports editor John Hunt accompanied me on the trip. There was an excellent bar walking distance from the hotel and we took advantage of it. The next morning, we sat out on the Marquis patio, enjoying our free buffet, when Hunt let go with a beer-fueled rat-a-tat-tat of flatulence. As if on cue, our waitress, who was of Asian descent, appeared out of nowhere and asked, in broken English, "Did you order eggs?"

We spent the rest of the day rolling up and down all of Atlanta's various Peachtree streets looking for vacancy signs. To our chagrin there was a Shriner convention in town. After checking out our seventh hotel, a concierge looked at us with a smirk as if to say, "Good luck, schmoes."

It was late afternoon and we were puttering through a boarded-up section of downtown. Across from a liquor store was a motel with a sign flashing the magic word: vacancy. The place did not take credit cards. There were bars on the windows. The rooms were $39 a night, or $10 an hour. Game time was looming.

We took it.

Over at Fulton County Stadium, Smith graciously talked to us on the sideline during the fourth quarter as kids on the front row clamored for a souvenir. Smith obliged, tearing off some athletic tape, balling it up and heaving it toward them. It was a nice gesture except he accidentally nailed an old woman on the forehead who wasn't paying attention.

After the postgame locker-room interviews, we were pleased to find that, in the NFL, unlike college, they serve free beer to the media. We had no deadline and were the last two people standing. The cleaning lady eventually asked us to leave.

After closing down The Beer Mug, we returned to our dive. It was about 4 a.m. and we were looking over our shoulders. There were pieces of wood missing from our door, and a new padlock had been bolted over it. It was pretty obvious the door, on some previous night, had been kicked in.

The blankets on the two twin beds were threadbare and frayed. The room reeked of second-hand smoke. Tiles were missing from the shower stall. And the worst thing of all, the TV didn't work.

We were stretched out on our beds when Hunt noticed something crawling up the cinderblock wall. It was a cockroach the size of an armadillo. Hunt took a glass ashtray from the nightstand and hurled it at the roach, nailing him. The roach shrugged it off and kept climbing.

The next morning we checked out, clutching our coupons. And I can say in full confidence we are the only two people in the history of the world to stay at that motel and then eat a free breakfast at the Marriott Marquis.

In 1987, an announced crowd of 10,500 braved the frigid cold to watch Tech wrap up its first football season under Frank Beamer with a 21-20 win at home over Cincinnati. After the game,

Collegiate Times sports editor John Hunt, SID Jack Williams, Hokies broadcaster Jeff Charles, videographer Steve Cohen, network assistant Ralph Stewart and I boarded a small prop plane for Tech's Big Apple Preseason NIT basketball game at Mufreesboro that night.

"You guys are really going to get on that little plane?" *Roanoke Times* reporter Blair Kerkhoff said. "Man, haven't you ever seen that movie, *The Buddy Holly Story?*"

Somehow, despite NCAA sanctions on the basketball team, loss of football scholarships and the firings of the athletic department's two most prominent coaches, the *Huddler* survived. Despite the bleak sports forecasts, there were enough die-hard Hokies out there buying subscriptions and advertising to help keep the thing afloat. The paper was still losing money, but it wasn't a lot of money, and for some reason the administration believed it still had a chance to turn a profit one day. I was still working seven days a week, however, and the long hours eventually took their toll.

The 1987 season had been a fiasco. The Hokies had just lost to West Virginia in Morgantown 28-16 to fall to 1-8. Everybody was in a lousy mood. Sunday morning I arrived at the *Christiansburg News-Messenger* (our new print site; no more *Galax!*) to begin the long production day. The newspaper office was windowless and reeked of second-hand smoke.

"How's that feature on Sean Donnelly coming along?" I asked part-time assistant John Hunt.

"Good. I'm still working on it."

Of course he was working on about 10 other things too. At around midnight, I reminded him about the story; he said it was almost done. We were both weary and bleary, and at about 3 a.m. I finally got to read the piece.

Donnelly, a senior fullback, was a character straight out of a Dan Jenkins novel: He smoked, he drank, he danced naked in the locker room. "I could give you some great Sean Donnelly stories," former safety Carter Wiley said, "but I don't think you could print any of them. He had an uncanny ability to make people absolutely throw up."

The story was a bit risqué, but at that hour, I wasn't about to have Hunt rewrite the thing. We finally left the newspaper office around 4 a.m.

The next day I picked up the *Huddlers* and distributed them around the Jamerson Athletics Center. It was about 6 p.m. when sports information director Jack Williams burst into my office.

"I can't believe you did this!" he said. "I can't believe you did this!"

"What, Jack, what?"

"This Sean Donnelly story. Coach Beamer is really upset about it. We might all lose our jobs over this. You've got to get all those papers and throw them out."

I pulled out a copy and reread the story.

Oh. I could see where the coach might be upset.

The next day, I woke at the crack of dawn and waited for the campus mail center to open. Then I took 10,000 *Hokie Huddlers* and threw them into the dumpster, bundle-by-bundle. We replaced the Donnelly piece with a story from the game program on lineman Greg Drew and paid for a new press run.

What I didn't know was that running backs coach Billy Hite called Donnelly at his apartment at 7:30 the previous night. "Don't move," he said. "I'm coming to pick you up."

Donnelly said the sight of Coach Hite at his door was "freaky." Hite didn't come in; he said, simply, "Let's go."

On the way up to Beamer's office, Hite said, "Look, this is about that article in the *Hokie Huddler*. It's out in print now and it's bad. It's really, really bad, and Coach Beamer is really upset."

"What do you mean?" Donnelly thought the worst of it was about smoking cigarettes. But it had the drinking and everything else in it.

Hite brought Donnelly into Coach Beamer's office and sat him down. The way Donnelly remembered it, the conversation went something like this: "Sean, you know, here you are, a senior," Beamer said. "You've been here five years, and I think you've been done a disservice. This article doesn't seem to match your personality, Sean, so I've got ask you a couple of questions. Do you smoke cigarettes?"

"No sir. There were some cigarettes on the table, and my roommates had some people over. They must have left one and I might have lit it as a joke."

"OK Sean. Now, do you drink beer during the season?"

"No sir."

Donnelly sweated through some more questions and then Beamer looked at him. "Well, we're not going to publish this. You've done too many things at this school to look bad in this article."

On the way home Hite looked at Donnelly and said, "What the [bleep] is the matter with you?"

Nearly 18 years later, Donnelly can laugh about it. "People always think I was mad at John for writing the article," he said. "I was never mad at him. I thought he actually did a really good job."

Adventure always seemed to follow John Hunt, who went from *Collegiate Times* sports editor to *Hokie Huddler* part-time assistant to *USA Today*. Today he's a sportswriter and columnist for the *Portland Oregonian*.

One Saturday morning he woke up with a raging hangover. Realizing he was late for the Hokies football game, he threw on some clothes and raced out the door. Fighting through the traffic, he couldn't find a place to park. The only spot open was the space reserved for Virginia Tech's No. 1 donor. Hunt shrugged and pulled his rusty blue 1981 Ford Escort wagon into the spot and rushed to the stadium, barely making the kickoff.

Needless to say, when he returned, his car had been towed.

The 10 Coolest Things About Lane Stadium/Worsham Field, circa 2002

1. The Hokies take the field by emerging from a limestone framed tunnel
2. Before they emerge, highlights from great past moments flash on the HokieVision board to the sound of Metallica's "Enter Sandman"
3. Turkey gobbling from the loudspeakers
4. Two band sections in the South End Zone (SEZ): Marching Virginians and Highty-Tighties
5. Limestone (aka "Hokiestone") walls in the south corners
6. Orange railings
7. H-O-K-I-E-S in maroon block letters on the press box façade
8. The Tree standing between the West stands and the North end zone, and the grassy knoll it stands on
9. Retired numbers poles
10. Concession stands selling barbecue turkey legs

At the 1994 Big East media day, I asked Miami All-America defensive tackle Warren Sapp if he knew the answer to the question, "What is a Hokie?"

"It's a bird," Sapp said. "Like a chicken hawk."

I told him the truth: that "Hokie" was just a made-up name from an 1896 cheer.

"Is that right?" Sapp said. "Well, they have somebody who runs around on the field in a bird costume. You tend to associate the nickname with the mascot."

A little later I had lunch with Sapp and Miami teammates Chris T. Jones and C.J. Richardson. Sapp was talking about eating somewhere on the road and how bad it was.

"I ordered Sloppy Joes," he said, "but they were Soybean Joes."

Lane Stadium, before it was cool.

Frank Beamer always mentions Tech's September 23, 1995 win over Miami (13-7) as a turning point for his program. Even though his team was coming off two consecutive bowl trips, he was feeling some pressure the week of that game. The Hokies had lost four in a row dating back to the previous season, including an embarrassing, turnover-marred home loss to rival Virginia 42-23 and a 35-23 shellacking at the hands of Tennessee in the Gator Bowl. In the off-season, Beamer lost both coordinators (Rickey Bustle went to South Carolina and Phil Elmassian went to Washington). The Hokies opened the '95 season with a 20-14 home loss to Boston College and a disappointing 16-0 loss at home against underdog Cincinnati. And now they were set to face the pass-happy Hurricanes without star cornerback Antonio Banks. Two true freshmen, Loren Johnson and Pierson Prioleau, would be filling in for him. I thought to myself, "Tech is going to get killed."

The Thursday before the game, I went down to visit with Beamer. We talked about scheduling philosophy. After he answered my questions I got up to leave, figuring he was busy preparing for the game, but he didn't get up. So I sat back down. I could tell he was frustrated. The week before, there had been heavy rain on Friday and Saturday morning, but there was a snafu and the field wasn't covered in time. By game time it was muck. "Before the game I walked out there and saw the condition of the field," he said, "and then I looked over at the Cincinnati team warming up. I saw those fat linemen they had, and I knew we were in for a struggle."

That Friday, the *Collegiate Times* ran the following classified ad: "Lost! Lost! Lost! Hokie football team. Last seen playing in the first half against Rutgers in November of 1994. Big reward if found."

Miami had beaten Tech by a combined score of 88-28 the previous three seasons, but the Hokies played inspired football. One of those freshmen cornerbacks, Johnson, broke up a fourth-down pass late in the game, and the Hokies won 13-7. I remember seeing Tech students swarming on top of the Big East TV truck, rocking it back and forth.

The Hokie team was found, and the reward was big indeed. Tech went on to win its next 10 games, including the 1995 Sugar Bowl in New Orleans against big, bad Texas.

CHAPTER TWELVE

Reveling in the Afterlife

Before the spring of 2003, sane Virginia Tech fans looked upon joining the ACC as pure fantasy. The Hokies' ardor toward the league was a long, painful story of unrequited love. It didn't matter that Tech was a nearly perfect fit for her on every level: geographically, academically, aesthetically, and spiritually. Or that the school, located squarely in the ACC's footprint, already had academic associations with three original ACC schools: Virginia (Carilion Biomedical Institute), Wake Forest (The Virginia Tech-Wake Forest University School of Biomedical Engineering and Sciences), and Maryland (Virginia-Maryland Regional College of Veterinary Medicine). To the ACC, Virginia Tech was somehow not worthy. When the league expanded in 1979, it invited Georgia Tech; when it grew again in 1991, it welcomed Florida State.

After years of football independence, the Hokies eventually found happiness when they joined the Big East in 1991. The team finally had a league title for which to fight, and with it, an automatic BCS berth. Without Big East affiliation, Virginia Tech would likely never have played for the 1999 national championship against Florida State.

"We were looking at national rankings the other day," said Raycom CEO Ken Haines. "Almost every school on that list has a long tradition of success. Virginia Tech is about the only one that achieved national prominence in the last few years. What it has accomplished is amazing."

But on April 17, 2003, even that relationship seemed on the brink of disaster—and the ACC was to blame. That was the day Big East commissioner Mike Tranghese ripped the ACC for trying to "conquer (the Big East) by dividing."

That's the day it became public: the ACC wanted to expand!

And it wanted three Big East teams!

And their names were Miami, Boston College—and Syracuse!

The news was a dagger in the collective hearts of Tech fans. How could this be? Miami, they could see; any league would crave a football powerhouse located in a tropical paradise outpost. But Syracuse and Boston College? One school was located in a professional sports-oriented city; the other was located near the Canadian border. And neither fan base sat around fantasizing over ACC membership. Even then-SU coach Paul Pasqualoni called a possible move "insane."

Tech would have given the ACC another national-caliber football program (and wasn't it football that was driving this thing?). Also, its fans were All-America travelers. Imagine the ticket sales at places such as Duke and Wake Forest, struggling to fill their stadiums, when the Hokies came calling. Travel for the league's Olympic sports teams would be so much cheaper and quicker than fighting the Northeast weather and traffic. Moreover, how many fans would Syracuse, Boston College, or Miami bring to those small college towns?

And don't even talk about TV ratings. Just ask ESPN what it thinks of Virginia Tech.

But it seemed the ACC refused to bear witness to logic. Instead, the Hokies became the odd man out, and it seemed the very foundation of their collegiate football success was about to be laid to waste.

For the next two months, the ACC expansion story took a new twist nearly every day. It was the stuff of Hollywood drama: closed-door intrigue, covert action, promises, lies, high-stakes agreements,

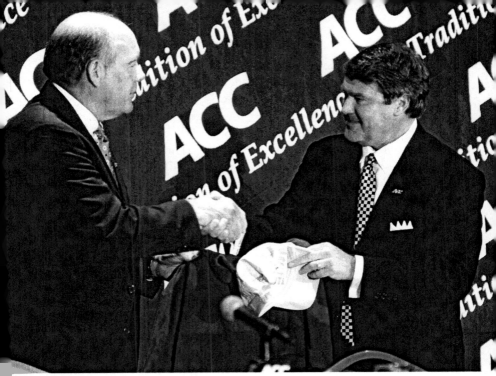

Virginia Tech Athletic Director Jim Weaver accepts ACC Commissioner John Swofford's invitation into the Atlantic Coast Conference.
Photo courtesy of David Knachel/Virginia Tech

power, greed, politics. Oh, and a multimillion-dollar lawsuit by five Big East schools—including Tech—against the ACC, Miami, and Boston College in an attempt to stop expansion.

Virginia Tech kept hearing ACC commissioner John Swofford talk about "entering new markets." What he forgot was that the ACC flourished largely because of its regional nature. The ACC thrived because it had a cluster of schools within a couple hours' drive of each other. The proximity, the familiarity, and the rivalry are precisely what made the league special.

The Roanoke Times sportswriter Doug Doughty related the story of South Carolina basketball coach Dave Odom, who spent 20 years in the ACC. "When I was at Wake Forest, if [Maryland coach] Gary Williams was playing golf, I knew about it," Odom said. "If Bobby Cremins [at Georgia Tech] was doing the ACC conference call from his hot tub, I knew about it. The thing that made the ACC unique was the intimacy." In the super-conference SEC, Odom said, it could be mid-May and he still wouldn't know what players Ole Miss had signed for the coming year. "They don't know anything about us, either," Odom said. "You lose the intimacy there."

Even former SEC commissioner Roy Kramer—who created this whole 12-team super-conference business back in 1991—questioned the ACC's thought process. "One of the things we looked at was homogenous institutions," he told ESPN.com's Ivan Maisel. "We wanted schools with a strong fan base that traveled well. TV wasn't a dominating factor. Our people were interested in fan base and a broad-based program. That drove our deliberations a lot more than TV markets. ...

"Do you create a rivalry with Boston College and North Carolina? I don't know how that works out. You put South Carolina in the mix with Georgia, Florida, and Tennessee, there's a certain geographical interest there. Do you get that same type of thing when you spread out? You have to speculate whether it will."

Ultimately, it all worked out for Virginia Tech. Virginia governor Mark Warner and attorney general Jerry Kilgore exerted political pressure on University of Virginia president John Casteen to protect Tech's interests. On June 27, 2003, Virginia Tech officially accepted the ACC's invitation. The Hokies, along with the University of Miami, officially joined the ACC on July 1, 2004, and a new era in Virginia Tech athletics was born.

Before the days of the internet, there was no Beamerball.com, Hokiesports.com, or TechSideline.com. For any fan in the Hokie epicenter and beyond, *The Roanoke Times* was THE news source.

And a columnist named Bill Brill wielded its greatest influence.

For 31 years until his 1991 retirement, Brill lent an air of national prestige to the paper as its executive sports editor. He knew pretty much anybody who was anybody in the world of collegiate athletics, and he served as president of the United States Basketball Writers Association in 1980-81. He was one of only a handful of voices in the Tech media world, and what he wrote seemed to matter oh so much.

His words, however, often upset Tech fans.

It was no secret Brill loved the ACC—particularly basketball. "But for some reason he didn't like Virginia Tech," said associate head coach Billy Hite. "When they made me play in those media golf tournaments, they always paired Brill with me. I guess they figured I was the only one who got along with him. And after being with him for 18 holes, I used to say, 'Aw, man, that guy ain't so bad.' Then I'd get up the next morning, read the paper, and go, 'Why, that (bleeper bleeper)!'"

Brill said he got along fine with most of the Tech coaches—but not all. "Frank Moseley was an SEC guy, and he and I disagreed on a lot of things," Brill said. "And I didn't get along with Bill Dooley. I didn't object to him at all as Dooley the football coach. But I did as Dooley the athletic director—and I proved to be accurate. It was a job he clearly wasn't qualified for. I remember talking to (basketball coach) Charlie Moir. He said he talked to Dooley twice the whole time he was there: the day Dooley arrived and the day (Charlie) retired. Dooley just wanted to promote his own agenda. He wanted a level playing field, and if you had to do something on the shaky side, well, that was OK with him. I used to tell him, 'Bill, you can talk all you want about leveling the playing field. But Notre Dame is still going to be Catholic, and Southern California is still going to be in Los Angeles.'"

That's the way it went. Each morning during the Brill reign, Tech athletics department staffers would fetch their copy of the *Times* with a sense of trepidation. "He's like water dripping on a stone," Dooley said of Brill. "Constantly eating away at you—drip, drip, drip."

Of course, when the Hokies deserved derision, Brill pounced with glee, or so it seemed to Tech fans.

"If I had a disagreement, it was with fans who wanted Frank Moseley, rah-rah-type journalism," Brill said. "Hey, I had problems with University of Virginia people, too. But if you're a columnist and you don't make somebody mad, you're probably not doing your job.

"The thing that soured a lot of people on me happened in 1979, when the ACC expanded and took Georgia Tech instead of

Virginia Tech. Obviously that decision was made to get the Atlanta television market. I wrote that the ACC made the right decision, because it was a business decision. I got more mail for that than anything I ever wrote, and some people never forgave me for it."

Some observers pooh-poohed the idea of any bias and brushed it off, proclaiming the Hokies too sensitive. "I don't think he arrived in Roanoke with any preconceived hatred for Virginia Tech," Doughty said. "But I do think he felt Tech fans had an inflated opinion of their sports teams."

Eventually some Hokies gave up trying to appease him—sometimes stooping to egregious behavior. Eschewing any pretense of professionalism, one mid-1980s headline in the student newspaper *The Collegiate Times* read, "Bill Brill, You Make Me Ill." At the 1986 Peach Bowl, Brill wore a peach-colored sports jacket, and while he worked the postgame locker room someone took a marker and scribbled a profanity on his back. One year Virginia Tech hosted a Metro Conference baseball game against Florida State at Salem Municipal Field. The stadium featured a tiny press box where writers could choose to watch from its roof. Brill stood at this vantage point when a group of fans below spotted him and yelled, "Jump!"

Even after he retired to Durham, North Carolina—where he now contributes to a Duke sports publication—Brill continued to jab Tech. After the Hokies joined their new conference, he predicted they would not win an ACC championship in his lifetime.

"Some Hokies stayed angry with Brill during his 30-year tenure as sports editor of *The Roanoke Times*," Doughty wrote in a July 1 column. "No doubt, he will make some new enemies with his latest pronouncement."

Of the quote, Brill said, "That was barroom talk, not for the paper. But it stemmed from the fact that, other than football, Tech wasn't very good in anything else. And I didn't realize Miami and Florida State would falter in football like they did."

Experts did not expect much from Virginia Tech in its inaugural ACC football season. In 2003 the Hokies finished a disappointing 8-5, losing four of their last five games, including a 52-49 heartbreaker to California in the Insight Bowl. And they lost five players selected in the 2004 NFL Draft: cornerback DeAngelo Hall (the eighth overall pick), running back Kevin Jones (No. 30), center Jake Grove (No. 45), wide receiver Ernest Wilford (No. 120), and defensive end Nathaniel Adibi (No. 145). The media picked Tech to finish sixth in the conference. Brill's prediction seemed safe.

For their first game as members of the ACC, the Hokies unveiled new Nike uniforms for their August 28 showdown against preseason No. 1 Southern California. Gone, blessedly, were the inexplicably mismatched orange sleeve numerals. Orange and maroon piping augmented the white jerseys—not garish, but enough to give the outfits a little more pizzazz. The Chicago maroon pants featured a slim strip of burnt orange down the side that flared behind the knee. The only quibble came with orange stockings so bright they almost made the fans in the upper deck squint. Didn't Nike know stockings were an NFL thing, and collegians were supposed to play with bare calves?

An 18-point underdog, Virginia Tech led 10-7 in the third quarter and was driving for another score when a controversial call changed the game's momentum. From the Southern Cal 44, quarterback Bryan Randall lofted a deep pass to a well-covered Josh Hyman. But Hyman stopped short, cut inside the Trojan defender, and snagged the pass for a 32-yard gain to the Trojan 12.

Whistle. Pass interference—on Hyman.

"That was the most bogus call I've ever witnessed," said defensive end Darryl Tapp, now with the Seattle Seahawks. "It was the turning point in the game. It just put a damper on everything."

The officiating crew was from the Southeastern Conference. After the game, Hite sent the tape to the SEC office and asked for a response.

"They admitted it was a bad call," Hite said. "Of course, they didn't change the final score."

USC sealed the win with 5:35 left in the fourth quarter. Quarterback Matt Leinart, who would win that year's Heisman Trophy, hit running back Reggie Bush on a wheel route for a 29-yard touchdown pass. Bush would win the Heisman in 2005.

Until he tore his biceps in the first half, linebacker Xavier Adibi had done a good job tracking Bush. Had he been in the game, could he have stopped that play?

"I will say this," defensive coordinator Bud Foster said. "They ran that wheel route earlier in the game. Xavier had Bush covered like a glove and Jim Davis sacked Leinart. When they ran it again, (reserve linebacker) Blake Warren was in for 'Zave.' He had a tough angle on Bush and got a little tripped up."

Despite the 24-13 loss, the day remains one of the most impressive in Virginia Tech history. The biggest crowd ever to see the Hokies—92,000 fans—filled FedEx Field in Landover, Maryland. "From a publicity standpoint, that game was huge," Tapp said. "When you have a cupcake to start the year, you might get a little lackadaisical. But because we opened with a powerhouse like USC, we had something to strive for. We worked hard the whole off-season, and (that) set the tone for the rest of the year."

Tapp brings up a good point, because many fans often underestimate the importance of what happens between January and July.

"We get a lot of credit for our victories," Hite said. "But a lot of it goes back to our strength coach, Mike Gentry. Players don't have time to get better during the season. The off-season is where you get better. And except for the 15 days of spring practice, Mike Gentry has those guys all spring and summer. I think that shows you how important our strength and conditioning program is here. I firmly believe that Mike Gentry makes our kids bigger, faster, and stronger."

Each week Foster awards Tech's famed lunch pail to the defender who scores the highest on the coaches' grade sheet. Tapp— nicknamed "Fast Forward" because of his tireless motor—won the pail in the season's first game and never relinquished it. "Until someone outworks me," Tapp said, "I'm keeping it."

After the Southern California game, Tapp told his teammates how proud he was of them, how they played hard, and how the young players stepped in and performed well. "Even though they didn't always play with the correct technique or fundamentals, they showed great character," he said.

But Tapp said one reporter tried to flip his words around. "He made it sound like we didn't care about winning games. That didn't sit well with me. I'm very respectful to all media people. But for someone to ask for an interview and then twist my words, I didn't appreciate that at all."

Tapp let his teammates read the article. "They weren't too thrilled about it," he said. "They knew where I was coming from and we used that as added motivation."

After pummeling Western Michigan (63-0 on September 11) and Duke (41-17 on September 18), the Hokies hosted N.C. State on September 25. The Wolfpack had the nation's top-ranked defense, led by 2006 NFL No. 1 pick Mario Williams, and played accordingly, sacking quarterback Bryan Randall 10 times for 78 yards in losses. This was one of the games that could have gone either way; State's two touchdowns came on drives of just 34 and five yards (the latter when Vinnie Burns dropped a punt snap).

Despite all that, the Hokies still had a chance to pull it out at the end.

"When we stopped N.C. State on its last drive, coach (Bud) Foster came up to each defensive player on the sideline," Tapp said. "He told us, 'Thanks for the effort. We did all we could do.' That's the first time I ever had a coach do that during a game."

With 2:44 left the Hokies took over at their own 6-yard line and, thanks to a 38-yard completion from Bryan Randall to David

Clowney on third-and-18, drove to the Wolfpack 24. But Brandon Pace's 43-yard field goal attempt sailed wide right as time expired.

"From my vantage point, I thought it was good," Tapp said. "Then I saw the N.C. State fans in the end zone jumping up and down."

The 17-16 loss dropped the Hokies to 2-2, and No. 6 West Virginia was next on the schedule. The Mountaineers had beaten Tech 28-7 the year before and rolled into Blacksburg on October 2 averaging 41.2 points.

"The key to the whole thing was the leadership we got from our head coach," Hite said. "Nobody panicked, and that's what is so special about Frank Beamer."

The Hokies didn't score an offensive touchdown, but defensive back Vinnie Fuller returned a blocked field goal for a touchdown and intercepted quarterback Rasheed Marshall. Tech's defense held WVU to 0-for-13 on third-down conversions. The Hokies beat WVU 19-13.

Virginia Tech's first-ever ACC road win came October 9 at Wake Forest—but it wasn't easy.

"There were a lot of games that year that could have gone either way," said tight end Jeff King. "That was one of them."

Quarterback Bryan Randall directed a 78-yard drive to give Tech a 17-10 lead with 2:10 to go, and then backup safety Mike Daniels batted down a Demon Deacon pass in the end zone on the game's last play.

"They ran a flanker delay and Mike sniffed it out," said assistant coach Jim Cavanaugh. "That was a good example of a kid, who wasn't a starter, coming through and making a big play."

"Fast Forward" Darryl Tapp kept the team's famed lunch pail the entire season.
Photo courtesy of David Knachel/Virginia Tech

After three consecutive stress-inducers, the Hokies finally got a breather on October 16 when they beat Florida A&M 62-0 in Blacksburg. The win marked the second time this season the Hokies outscored an opponent by at least 62 points.

Tech was in scoring position and held a 28-0 lead when an official threw a flag as time expired.

"The half can't end on a penalty!" a fan in section five exclaimed. "We can kick a field goal!"

The guy in front of him turned around and said, "It's only the end of the first quarter, you idiot."

The fan, who had been tailgating since early in the morning, looked at the scoreboard then said, "Well, it FEELS like halftime."

With Atlanta Falcons Michael Vick, Keion Carpenter, Kevin McCadam, and DeAngelo Hall looking on from the sidelines and a Thursday night ESPN audience watching across the country, Virginia Tech won a 34-20 thriller at Georgia Tech on October 28.

The Hokies were down 20-12 but scored 22 points in the final 5:28 minutes, marking their first comeback road win since 1995 (over Virginia).

Quarterback Bryan Randall hit wide receiver Eddie Royal for 80 yards and Josh Morgan for 51, and defensive back Roland Minor returned an interception 64 yards with less than a minute to play.

But linebacker Xavier Adibi made perhaps the game's most memorable play.

The Yellow Jackets, leading 17-12, had the ball on the Hokies' 5-yard line. On second down quarterback Reggie Ball dropped back to pass. Adibi, playing his first game since tearing his biceps against Southern California, sacked Ball for a 12-yard loss. One Techsideline.com poster likened the play to "a cheetah tracking down a gazelle on the open plain." Georgia Tech would settle for a field goal, its last points of the game.

"That was a huge play," Tapp said, "because Ball had been beating us bad on the bootleg, sucking the ends in with a long fake hand-off to running back. Every time we'd veer in to stop the run, he'd pull out the ball and run. And when we stayed out to cover the bootleg, he'd hand it off. As defensive ends, we started second-guessing ourselves."

After upsetting No. 4 Miami the week before, North Carolina was all fired up for the visiting 18th-ranked Hokies on November 6. For most of the game, however, Tech was in control, leading 27-14 with 3:10 left in the third quarter. Running back Mike Imoh rushed for a school-record 243 yards.

UNC trimmed a 27-14 VT lead to 27-24 with two late scores, but Carolina kicker Connor Barth missed a 54-yard field goal attempt with just over a minute remaining.

End Jim Davis made the defensive play of the game, sacking senior quarterback Darian Durant for an 11-yard loss. Otherwise Barth would've been attempting a more makeable 43-yard field goal.

Frank Beamer has enjoyed many great wins in his Virginia Tech career. But none came on a sadder day than November 18. His mother, Herma, died that morning. Her last wish to her son's players was simple: Beat Maryland.

"Everybody on the staff just let Coach be," assistant Jim Cavanaugh said. "We tried to make everything as normal as we possibly could."

And Beamer's players did as they were told. No. 15 Tech beat the Terrapins 55-6.

Sure, their games are televised on ESPN and they get their pictures in the paper. But life as a college football player isn't always glamorous.

Tapp shared an apartment with linebacker James Anderson. And the thing about roommates is, you never know when they're going to raid your stuff.

One night Tapp ordered a pizza and ate half. The next day he went to class, all morning thinking he would have the rest of that pizza for lunch. "I had my mind set on it," he said.

But when he arrived home, he took out the box only to find it empty.

"James," he said, "did you eat my pizza?"

"Oh yeah," Anderson said. "I meant to tell you about that."

In the Commonwealth of Virginia, the annual Virginia Tech-Virginia game was always a big deal. But now, for the first time, the game had added importance: it was an ACC league game.

And there was plenty on the line. Both teams were 8-2. With a win Tech, ranked No. 11, would clinch at least a tie for the ACC title. UVA, ranked 16th, would earn a share of the ACC title and retain a slim chance of winning the league's BCS berth.

The Hokies had added motivation: they wanted to atone for a 35-21 loss in Charlottesville the year before, a game in which tight end Heath Miller caught 13 passes for 145 yards.

November 27 marked the last home game for 19 Tech seniors, including quarterback Bryan Randall. He made his last Lane Stadium appearance a memorable one, completing 16 of 22 passes for 200 yards, two touchdowns, and no interceptions. In the second half he completed 10 of 12 passes for 141 yards in Tech's 24-10 win.

In a fit of euphoria, defensive coordinator Bud Foster tackled rover James Griffin. "He jumped on me and I took advantage of the opportunity," Foster said. "Those guys are getting too big and strong for me, so I have to get leverage to bring them down these days."

The win set the stage for a showdown with old Big East rival Miami. Oh, the irony: the two league newcomers playing for the ACC title.

Running back Kevin Jones missed out on all the fun of 2004; he opted to enter the NFL draft. But when you begin talking Miami, he gets all misty eyed.

"My fondest memory at Tech was beating Miami 35-7 in Lane Stadium," Jones said. "They were at the top of their game, and I guaranteed the win before the game."

Jones was the highest-profile recruit ever at Virginia Tech; some services rated him the nation's No. 1 prospect. "It's kind of funny, because (the Hokies) didn't really recruit me. I recruited them," Jones said. "I was down there for a track meet. I stopped off at the football office and gave them a highlight tape. It kind of started from there. I was the one who initiated the relationship."

Jones had hoped to play with quarterback Michael Vick, who ended up turning pro after his sophomore season. But he said the Tech coaches also played a big role in his decision. "I felt a great family atmosphere," he said, "and I knew I had the opportunity to play early."

That opportunity came in the second game of his freshman year, 2001. Starter Lee Suggs suffered a knee injury in the season opener against Connecticut, and Hite, Tech's running backs coach, worked overtime with Jones to ensure he understood all of the protection schemes.

Hite felt comfortable that Jones knew what he was supposed to do. During the following day's running backs film session, Hite asked Jones, who was sitting behind him, about his blocking assignment.

Silence.

Again, Hite said, "Kevin, on this play, who are you supposed to block?"

No answer.

"Turn on the light!" Hite screamed, and that's when Jones woke from his nap.

"You (bleeper bleeper)!" Hite said more than once. "Get out of here NOW!"

Said Jones, "It had been a long day after practice and the meeting room didn't have any windows. It was dark and the film was playing. I couldn't help it. He called me a few choice words that I'm not going to repeat."

But in a later meeting, Jones enjoyed a measure of revenge. Hite called out Jones' name. Jones remained motionless. Hite tried again when Jones, who had been feigning sleep, leaped from his desk and said, "I GOT you this time!"

The two still joke about the incident. Jones will sometimes call Hite and greet him, "How are you doing, you (bleeper-bleeper)?"

And so on December 4, the No. 10 Hokies traveled to Miami to take on the ninth-ranked Hurricanes in an ABC-televised game. It promised to be a close one; analyst Gary Danielson said the teams could switch jerseys and, but for a few exceptions, you could not tell them apart.

The week before, TV cameras caught James Griffin holding a marker board that said "ACC Champs." Miami players did not appreciate the presumptive gesture. ESPN analyst Kirk Herbstreit called Griffin's stunt "a mistake" and picked the Hurricanes to win.

As expected, the game was close. With the score tied at 10 in the fourth quarter, quarterback Bryan Randall executed a sweet play-action fake and hit wide receiver Eddie Royal on a crossing pattern. Royal stretched and caught the ball on his fingertips ahead of All-America candidate Antrel Rolle, who would be the No. 8 pick in the

Coach Frank Beamer raises his arms in triumph as the Hokies beat Miami for the ACC Championship. *Photo courtesy of David Knachel/Virginia Tech*

2005 NFL draft. Royal left Rolle in the dust for the go-ahead score with 11:29 to play, but Miami blocked the extra point.

The 'Canes had three more possessions in the game, but the Hokie defense stopped them each time. Tech sealed the win when it batted down three consecutive Brock Berlin passes, two by Jim Davis and the last by Tapp.

With the 16-10 win, the Hokies won the ACC Championship outright at a 7-1 mark, earning the right to play in the Sugar Bowl against No. 3 Auburn—a Tigers team that would have four players taken in the first round of the 2005 NFL draft: running backs Ronnie Brown (No. 2 overall) and Cadillac Williams (the No. 5 overall pick), cornerback Carlos Rogers (No. 9), and quarterback Jason Campbell (No. 25).

Billy Hite has been coaching football in Blacksburg since 1978, first as part of Bill Dooley's staff and then with Frank Beamer. Perhaps no man is better qualified to put Virginia Tech's football exploits in perspective, and he rated the 2004 Miami win the second-most important in his tenure.

No. 1 would have to be the first time the Hokies beat the Hurricanes, in 1995.

A 16-0 loss to Cincinnati left the Hokies 0-2, and the Tech staff gathered for their weekly Sunday night meeting, awaiting Beamer with great trepidation. No. 17 Miami was next, a team Virginia Tech had never beaten. The three previous seasons, the Hurricanes had beaten the Hokies by a combined score of 88-28.

"I never thought we would ever beat Miami," Hite said.

Beamer walked in at 9 p.m. and calmly scanned the room. "Our players want to win," he said. "Put them in the best possible position to beat Miami."

And then he got up and walked out.

The Tech assistants sat and looked at each other. "If I was him," Hite said, "I would have fired every (bleeping) guy sitting in there, because I could have coached as well as those (bleeping) nine guys did all by myself."

But the bleeping coaches executed their coach's order that week, and the Hokies beat Miami 13-7.

"Some people say beating Texas in the Sugar Bowl was our biggest game, or playing in the national championship game against Florida State," Hite said. "There have been a lot of big games, don't get me wrong. But that 1995 Miami game, to me, is still the most important game we've ever won at Virginia Tech. That win set the tone for our football program."

After the Miami game, the team awarded Foster the game ball. He still considers that the greatest honor of his career, even though he would win the 2005 Frank Broyles Award as the nation's top NCAA Division I assistant coach. Considering the sheer number of collegiate assistant coaches in the country, that's a tremendous accomplishment.

The engraved 60-pound trophy arrived at the Jamerson Athletic Center on February 28, 2007. "My office is actually too small for it," Foster said. "We might have to display it somewhere else."

A former Murray State linebacker, Foster still harbors a fiery side—something even the offensive players hear, regardless of whether they see it. "Every Friday the team would gather in our main meeting room, and they'd split it up with a divider: offense on one side, defense on the other, discussing the game plan," said center Will Montgomery. "And at least once a week, we could hear Coach Foster screaming through the divider. Sometimes we would stop our meeting for a few seconds just to listen."

Said Foster, "There might be some truth to that. I might read a quote one of the opposing players said about our program. If we needed to create a crisis, then I'd create a crisis."

Tight end Jeff King had one of the most interesting careers of any Tech athlete. He was a key starter on an ACC Championship football team and played on a Hokies basketball team that upset a Duke team ranked seventh in the nation. When asked about his fondest collegiate sports memories, he ranked winning at Miami No. 1, playing in the Sugar Bowl No. 2, and beating the Blue Devils No. 3.

"The play everybody remembers is when I hit the hook shot over (center) Shelden Williams," King said. "So that's something I can always go back to."

Virginia Tech's win at Miami sent Hokie fans rushing to their phones and computers, scrambling to gain flights and prime New Orleans hotel accommodations. Meanwhile, ACC commissioner John Swofford—a former teammate of Billy Hite's at North Carolina—visited Tech's jubilant postgame locker room, putting into words what Virginia Tech knew all along.

"You have brought an amazing energy to the ACC," he said. "The team, and the way the fans come out to visiting stadiums, it just stimulates the other schools."

When the football team arrived in Blacksburg that evening, the party was in full swing. A fire truck, with lights flashing and siren screaming, met the Hokie busses and led them to Cassell Coliseum.

"We saw all these cars in the parking lot," Tapp said. "I don't know how they organized it so fast."

Athletics department officials ushered the team onto the Cassell Coliseum floor as Metallica's "Enter Sandman" blared and 8,000 fans cheered. "I'll never forget it," said Montgomery. "Whenever I hear that song, I think of screaming fans and I always get an adrenaline rush. It just triggers a feeling. Even now, when I'm driving around in my car and that song comes on, I get goose bumps."

That night Tapp returned to his apartment exhausted. The Miami game temperature had been in the mid-70s, and the visitor's bench was in the sunlight. "Miami was in the shade," he said. "By the end of the game, we were running on fumes."

He felt exhausted—but euphoric. In their first year of ACC competition, the Hokies were league football champions.

"We definitely felt a sense of vindication," Tapp said. "It was like a dream come true."

A dream come true for the players—and also Hokie fans everywhere.

"For all those years, we were in the heart of ACC country and had to hear all that talk about us being a stepchild," Foster said. "So to go win the championship in our first year in the league, that was special."

Oh, and Brill? Despite his pronouncement that Virginia Tech would not win an ACC championship in his lifetime, when the Hokies hoisted the ACC title trophy, he was still alive and well.

Epilogue

Although this book was largely a collection of humorous anecdotes, it seems fitting to end it with a story that embodies the Hokie spirit.

When senior associate athletic director Sharon McCloskey was an undergraduate in the 1970s, she took a summer job working on the athletics department grounds and maintenance crew. She was putting herself through college, and the job paid more than minimum wage.

Her day began at 7:30 a.m., with a half-hour break for lunch. One of her first jobs was to shovel a pile of sand onto a trailer. After watching McCloskey work, supervisor Buford Meredith asked her if he could make a suggestion without her getting mad at him.

"Sure, Buford," she said. "Why would I get mad?"

"Well, if you would hold your shovel closer to the blade," he said, "you'll make things easier on yourself."

McCloskey was starting to have second thoughts about her job, thinking, "You wouldn't think a person would need instructions on how to use a shovel, but I guess I do."

At lunchtime McCloskey pulled out her peanut butter sandwich. Being a college student, she couldn't even afford jelly.

After about 30 seconds she was finished. Meredith saw this and offered her some of his chips and cookies. Then he began bringing her an extra sandwich. Then a sandwich and an extra bag of chips.

In a few weeks, he went from bringing a brown bag to a grocery bag—and most of it was for McCloskey. Even with the extra food, she lost 30 pounds that summer.

She earned her degree and eventually took a job in the football office. She worked her way up from secretary to recruiting coordinator to one of the top spots in the athletics department, where one of her responsibilities during Tech home games is taking care of the officials. She makes their hotel reservations and orders their gameday food.

A few years ago she went into Lane Stadium's workshop to eat her pregame meal with Meredith. But someone had miscalculated the order, or perhaps another worker took more than their share. Either way, there was no meal for Meredith. McCloskey offered to share her sandwich, but he wouldn't hear of it.

The next game day McCloskey added one more item to her checklist. When she ordered the officials' food she included two extra meals—and had them delivered to one of the stadium security guards with explicit instructions to hold it for her.

Now, before every game, McCloskey picks up the meals and heads to the stadium shop. She and Meredith talk over many things, some important, some not so important.

After 40 years on the Virginia Tech grounds crew, things for Meredith had come full circle.

Where he once fed a hungry student, that former student now feeds him.

Celebrate the Heroes of Football
in These Other New and Recent Releases from Sports Publishing!

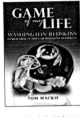

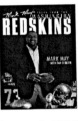

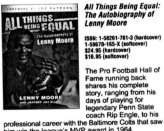

Printed in the United States
87794LV00002B/154-1104/A